CONVERSATIONS
WITH WINEMAKERS
MENDOZA, ARGENTINA

Grape Collective

Grape Collective Publishing
A division of Grape Collective
2669 Broadway, New York, NY 10025

Edited by Christopher Barnes
Interviews by Christopher Barnes, Dorothy J. Gaiter
Photography by Christopher Plante

MENDOZA
ARGENTINA

CONTENTS

09 David Bonomi
Bodega Norton PAGE 70

01 An Introduction to
Mendoza PAGE 6

10 Gustavo Arizu
Luigi Bosca PAGE 74

02 José Alberto Zuccardi
Zuccardi PAGE 14

11 Max Toso
Huarpe PAGE 80

03 Gerardo Michelini
Zorzal PAGE 22

12 Facundo Pereira
Casa Bianchi PAGE 86

04 Paul Hobbs
Los Cabos PAGE 28

13 Aurelio Montes Jr.
Kaiken PAGE 90

05 José Galante
Salentein PAGE 34

14 Up & Coming Winemakers
The next generation PAGE 100

06 Daniel Pi
Trapiche PAGE 44

15 Eat and Sleep
Where to dine and stay PAGE 104

07 Ernesto Bajda
Catena Zapata PAGE 54

16 Outside of Mendoza
Wine regions PAGE 108

08 Ana Balbo
Dominio del Plata PAGE 62

ACKNOWLEDGMENTS

While the title is Conversations with Winemakers, the focus of this book is to interview people who are part of a region's wine story, and this includes winery owners, industry insiders as well as chefs. During our trip to Mendoza, the passionate winemakers, owners and chefs who I spoke to were very giving of their time and very honest in their assessments about the reasons behind the success of Malbec.

Many people helped to created this book. The team at Wines of Argentina who were extremely helpful in coordinating our visits. Thanks go to the winemakers of Mendoza who were so giving of their time. Special thanks to the co-pilot on the project, Alfonso Nogueroles, who traveled across the world and put up with a lot of craziness. Bruce Kuo and Christopher Sabatini for their design input. Barbara Vyden and Rachael Doob for their help in proofreading. Michael Woodsmall for his editing skills. Also I would like to thank Nancy Hay, Clara Maxine, Maxim R. Duckworth, Dorothy J. Gaiter and Joshua Aranda for their support of the Grape Collective project. Lastly, I'm grateful for the wonderful energy provided by the team of writers contributing to Grape Collective who make the project fun to be a part of.

AN INTRODUCTION TO
Mendoza

Introduction

Driving down a dirt road in Luyan de Cuyo, Mendoza, an hour and a half late for our appointment, I'm still making sense of the traffic ticket I just received. Additionally, there is no signage for the wine estate we are visiting. Nor cell phone service. And the car is without GPS. The dry creek bed we are about to cross has boulders as big as soccer balls; we wince as they clang against the bottom of the car. Difficult to believe we are on our way to visit one of Argentina's most talked-about new wineries.

To those accustomed to vino-tourism in the United States, Argentina is a radically different experience—to quote Seinfeld, it's "an enigma, a mystery wrapped in a riddle."

In fact, Mendoza is the anti-Napa. There are no limos teeming with bachelorettes floundering among these dirt roads and dry creek beds of Mendoza. Frontier-like, there is a grit about the place. It is also full of contradictions: it is at once both a very new wine region as well as a very old wine region.

The History

Argentina has been making wine for centuries and has long been one of the highest per capita consumers of wine in the world. Yet it wasn't until the mid-eighties that it became an international wine sales powerhouse—almost out of nowhere—with Malbec as the star.

To better understand the country's history in wine, a story that began in the sixteenth century, it is necessary to first understand the people who make up the nation.

The new Zuccardi winery in the Uco Valley, Mendoza

In 1561, Spanish conquistadors trekked from Chile over the Andes into Argentina, bringing with them wine grapes. But the grapes alone were not enough. They needed an irrigation network, one they would borrow from the indigenous Huarpe. And with that, the conquistadors began making wine.

The Spanish crown, however, was not keen to encourage the evolution of the industry, as its goal was to export Spanish wine to the colonies. As with the irrigation network, the conquistadors made do with what was accessible. The original grapes that were planted in Argentina were Pais grapes, a variety indigenous to the Canary Islands of Spain. Later in the 1850s, the Mendoza government brought over a French viticulturist—the viticulturist responsible for bringing over the now pervasive and popular Bordeaux varietals, including Malbec.

Despite the growth of the local industry, the colonies continued to face challenges, most pressing being the challenge of transporting wines from Mendoza to Buenos Aires. As a result, local wine played second fiddle to cheaper and higher-quality imported wines from France.

7

Lamas at the Trapiche winery

But not for long. The creation of the Mendoza-to-Buenos Aires railway in 1885 provided a real spark, one that ignited the Argentine wine industry. And that spark was once again lit by immigrants, mostly of Italian descent who used the railway to settle in Mendoza. As with the Spaniards before them, these immigrants brought with them Old World winemaking skills. They also carried the understanding and will to expand the irrigation network. Above all, they introduced a new population of wine drinkers—their fellow immigrants. At one point, the per capita consumption in Argentina was as high as 90 liters per capita, which compared to the United States' 10 liters per capita is extremely high. It should be noted, however, that the overall improvement of "native" Argentine wines wasn't without aid: the vine destroying aphid phylloxera decimated 40% of French vines between the 1850s and 1870s. This put a dent in French imports and allowed the local industry an opportunity to showcase its wines.

The modern history of the Argentinian wine industry is heavily influenced by the boom and bust nature of local politics. Key players were Hector and José Greco, brothers who built a wine empire that at its height in the 1970s controlled nearly half of the Argentine wine market. The Grecos, an immigrant family, began in the wine business in Argentina in the late 1940s. Gradually, they took over many of the other larger immigrant family wine businesses, and in 1979 they bought Argentina's largest winery, Grupo Catena, from family

8

head Nicolás Catena. But their luck soon ran out. In 1980, a banking collapse caused a run on banks and resulted in the Grecos defaulting on their loans. As a result, the entire Argentine wine industry was almost wiped out.

Fortunately for the future of the Argentine wine industry, Nicolás Catena came out of the crisis relatively unscathed, and he was able to take back his company from the Grecos.

Catena and the Rise of Malbec

A central character in the rise of Argentine Malbec, Nicolás Catena is described by Evan Goldstein in his book Wines of South America as "the undisputed patriarch of Argentinean fine wine." In 1965 he inherited a family winery that was started by his grandfather Nicola in 1902. A trained economist, he was a visiting professor at Berkeley in the early 1980s when he encountered Robert Mondavi and the California push that took on the French which ultimately led to the famous victory at the Judgment of Paris in 1976. Catena came to understand and appreciate inconsistencies in the quality of winemaking, and how Argentina needed to improve its equipment, viticulture, and winemaking skills. In an interview with Decanter Magazine in 2009 he spoke to the experience: "We visited Robert Mondavi and tasting his wines was a shock. I loved the fruit and freshness of the Fumé Blanc, and the Cabernet Sauvignon, although young, was so full of fruit, aroma and flavour. It was a revelation."

As one of the few winemakers who had capital after the banking collapse, Catena invested in improving his wine operation. He hired American winemaker Paul Hobbs to consult and assist in his vision for quality. In an interview with Grape Collective's Dorothy J. Gaiter, Hobbs talked about the early days with Catena and how he discovered the great potential of Malbec. Hobbs explained that Catena originally wanted to focus on Chardonnay and Cabernet and had little regard for Malbec.

"Nicolás Catena had an old vineyard, a 100-year-old vineyard in a little area called Lunlunta along the Rio Mendoza River," he said. "I asked Nicolás if he would help finance some experimental trials with the grape. [Nicolás initially] said, 'No, the French have already demonstrated. They did not replant after phylloxera. They have already demonstrated as well, documented in the literature about this grape, so we're not going to invest in Malbec.' Nevertheless, his head viticulturist humored me and we began working on a section of the vineyard to grow the grapes in a way that I needed them grown."
"That old vineyard inspired me and so even against Nicolás' wishes I

proceeded."

The wines Hobbs made from that old vine Malbec garnered strong scores with the US—and thus the rise in Malbec began, Catena at the forefront of the export boom.

What defines the Malbec success also touches on the ability to produce value-priced wines coupled with undeniably smart marketing. Trapiche is able to produce a sub-$8 Malbec that provides hard-to-beat value at that price point. Likewise, in 1999, Susana Balbo built (from scratch) a wine business with her Crios and Ben Marco brands, employing a similarly aggressive business model. The theme? The wines are solid, easy to drink, and consistently good value.

Catena, headed by winemaker Pepe Gallante, was influential in the move to high altitude farming, which defines quality Malbec today and led to a new generation of Argentine wine innovators. His 1993 planting of the Adrianna vineyard in Gualtallary in the Uco Valley, 4757 feet above sea level was prescient.

The Evolution to a "Modern" Balanced Malbec

When one visits a European country, there is often debate between modern and traditional winemaking. "Modern" is used to describe a more fruit-forward high alcohol style that appeals to an international palate. In Argentina, the opposite is the case: "traditional" refers to the big, bold, fruity, high alcohol Malbec's that originally grabbed the attention of the American consumers and critics; "modern" refers to a more balanced, restrained style of winemaking with lower alcohol levels. The Uco Valley is where this so-called modern trend is taking off, with Zorzal at the forefront of this new movement and the Michelinis representing the new frontiersmen.

The Michelinis launched their winery in a barren, isolated part of the Uco Valley called Gualtallary. Giving up jobs, they set out to start a crazy project in a crazy place with the idea of building something unique and special. And they have succeeded. Their wines have layers of complexity absent in many of the more traditional Malbecs. They ferment their wines in concrete amphorae similar to those used in ancient times. The amphorae have been so successful that many of the Uco Valley winemakers have taken their lead, and now also use the vessels. Instead of importing the costly vessels from France, the Michelinis worked alongside a local fabricator to build them. Gerardo Michelini joked that he should have put a patent on the casks, as the fabricator now has a tremendous business building them for other winemakers.

The Trapiche winery

It is not just the small guys who are embracing the new style. José Alberto Zuccardi, owner of one of the largest wineries by volume in Argentina, has invested tremendous resources to build a winery in the Uco Valley, dedicated to making "modern" terroir -driven wines. In contrast to the Michelinis, he is using his considerable resources to invest in scientific studies, including complex soil mapping. They harvest and separate grapes based on soil type zones, rather than the traditional method of pulling vines from distinct vine rows.

Argentina has a number of challenges as a wine industry. First, there is its reliance on a single varietal and the risk of it falling out of fashion as Shiraz did in Australia. There are also the hurdles of the boom bust economic cycles in the country. Winemakers are faced with an asset wine that requires aging amidst tremendous inflation and the obstacles of dealing with an artificially inflated currency.

Mendoza is a complex region. It has a long history of winemaking and yet is a very modern creation. It is a story of international winemaking, strong marketing, and big success stories. The new wave of "modern" Mendoza winemakers are making bold, complex wines. As pioneering

The cement eggs at the new Zuccardi winery in the Uco Valley, Mendoza

winemaker José Gallante told Grape Collective about the potential of the Uco Valley and "modern" Argentine wines: "For me, it's exciting to think of the future and what will happen with this grape when it is 20, 30 years old. Maybe the quality will be amazing because now the young plants produce a very nice quality of grape, imagine what could happen in 10, 15 years ahead. In the future, I think this area could be fantastic."

Travel

Mendoza is a terrific destination for those with a sense of adventure. Travel is not easy. The simplest way to get to Mendoza is to fly into Santiago, Chile and either fly over the Andes, take a bus, or rent a car. We elected to take a bus yet ran into problems when LAN, the main Chilean airline, didn't send our luggage on our flight; we ended up missing our transport. LAN has a 30-minute flight to Mendoza, but it cost nearly as much as the ticket from New York. Despite losing our luggage, we were not offered a discount on the ticket.

Renting a car is also a challenge. It takes four days to process the insurance certificate required to cross the border into Argentina—so if you want to rent, it is wise to plan ahead. The night bus that we were forced to take is a rough ride. The drive itself is about four bumpy hours, and you are forced to stop and go through customs, which can take up to an additional two hours. During the day, the scenery through the Andes is a very pleasant, inspiring experience.

The other challenge with Mendoza is dealing with the government-regulated exchange rate. While at the hotel we were advised that if we went to the black market exchange, our hotel would cost 20% less. It is a strange experience loitering in front of a McDonald's then locating our black market money dealer and going down some stairs into a closed shop, and sitting down to count and exchange large stacks of money. It felt like a drug deal, and a very odd way to pay for a room at a large internationally known hotel.

Books on Argentine wine:

Evan Goldstein's Wines of South America
Laura Catena's Vino Argentino
Ian Mount's The Vineyard at the End of the World

JOSÉ ALBERTO ZUCCARDI
ZUCCARDI

Innovation is usually the bailiwick of the small aggressive start-up. The two guys in the garage rather than the big successful established company. Zuccardi is that rarity that can straddle both worlds. The company that has climbed to the top, but is still able to act like the two guys in the garage - only with greater resources.

Wine critic Jancis Robinson writing in the *Financial Times* dedicated a whole laudatory column to describing their success: "Their story incorporates mid 20th-century technical innovation, enviable sales success around the turn of the century and, now, a possible blueprint for the future of Argentine wine."

The story starts with Alberto Zuccardi's family emigrating from Italy to Argentina in the late 19th century. An engineer by trade, Alberto Zuccardi was responsible for helping to develop the irrigation system in Mendoza, which is essentially a desert. In 1963, Alberto Zuccardi planted the first acre of vines in Maipú, Mendoza. His son José Alberto is the force that made Zuccardi one of the top five exporters of Argentinian wines. They created a wine called Fuzion, a sub-$8 Malbec-Syrah blend which became the top selling wine in Canada. According to Ian Mount's book *The Vineyard at the End of the World*, in 2010 Zuccardi exported $40 million of wine, including 900,000 cases of Fuzion.

Yet even while the revenue was coming in from the inexpensive Malbec, the Zuccardis still had one eye on innovation. In her book *Vino Argentino*, Laura Catena praises José Alberto for the development of an experimental vineyard "where the winemakers have planted more than 35 varieties including obscure ones such as Caladoc, Bourboulenc Ancellota and Ekigaina - to study their adaptation to the conditions in Mendoza."

14

Today, Sebastián Zuccardi, a third generation winemaker, is taking the push to innovation even farther as the company strives to create more terroir-driven, vineyard specific wines. He oversees the research and development division of the company in the Uco Valley.

In recent wine history, technology has typically been used to create industrial, international style wines, but the Zuccardis are employing hi-tech techniques such as sophisticated soil mapping, to better develop their artisanal, terroir-focused winemaking. The soil mapping leads to the vines being picked and separated relative to their soil types rather than strict geographical proximity.

The new winery being built is state of the art, and yet a throwback at the same time. The wines being made are kept in concrete vats rather than wood or stainless steel. The resulting wines are imbued with more character, higher acidity, and are a far cry from the rich, oaky Malbecs we are used to and on which Argentina and the Zuccardis built their business.

We talk to José Alberto about the family history, the rise of the Uco Valley, and terroir winemaking.

José Alberto, tell us about how your family got into the wine business.

It's a nice story. My father was a civil engineer and he had a factory where he did a lot of prefabricated concrete pipes. He adapted some irrigation systems to our region that were used in 1950 in California. You know Mendoza is a desert. We cultivate just 3 1/2% of the surface of the province, and the limitation is the water that only comes from the melting of the snow on top of the Andes. He started with his irrigation system, and to show other producers how his irrigation system worked, he planted the vineyard. He became passionate about it. He was a real agriculture person. After five years he started building the original winery from the family in Maipú. I joined the project in 1976. Now we are three generations working together because my mother is still part of the team. She's 89, but still involved. I have three children and all of them are involved.

The Uco Valley is known for having wines that have a bit more structure and a bit more acidity than wines from other areas in Mendoza. How is that reflected through the soils that you have here?

I think the differentiation of the Uco Valley is that it's a region west of Mendoza next to the Andes Mountains, and here we are cultivating between 1000 meters, or about 3000 feet, until 1500 meters. That is 4500 feet. It is the highest altitude region in the Mendoza province.

The altitude means a lot and also because Mendoza is a desert, we have very low humidity. Rainfall here is six or seven inches a year. It means we have a big difference between the maximum and the minimum temperature everyday. This big difference in temperature and the amount of sunlight give the possibility to obtain grapes with a very good level of ripeness, but at the same time with a very good level of natural acidity because during the day it's hot, but during the night the temperature decreases a lot.

Everything here is related to the mountains, because the mountains determine the weather as they prevent the humid air coming from the Pacific Ocean. The mountains give us the soil, and alluvial movements made the soil. The only water we have for irrigation originates from the mountains.

In Mendoza, we irrigate 3 1/2% of the total surface of Mendoza, as 96.5% of Mendoza is desert and mountains. The only water we have

comes from the melting of the snow on top of the Andes. The other thing that the mountains give us is the altitude. The character of our wine comes from the Andes.

Altamira is part of an alluvial cone. We did a very intense study together with the university and we have defined this area. The main characteristic of this area is the predominance of calcium carbonate, good chalk in the soil. You can see the stones here. You can recognize the alluvial soils because all the stones are round. They came rolling down.

We started to study and we wondered where the calcium carbonate, all this chalk, comes from. Normally, it comes from the bottom of the sea. Many, many years ago, more than 100 million years ago, this area was at the bottom of a sea. After that, two plates went against each other and the Andes emerged. What was the bottom of a sea is now the top of the Andes.

What we found from this map tells us about what is underground. Then we started doing more detailed work, taking areas of vineyards

17

and dividing them depending on what is on the surface, what is deeper down, and the characteristics of the soil.

We started dividing our vineyard areas into different terroirs. This differentiation also means different ripening times for the grapes and different characteristics of the grapes.

How many different types of soils do you have here? You talked a little bit about the chalk, but what other soils?

Mainly this area in Altamira, there are alluvial soils with a lot of stones at different depths. In some places, the stones are on the surface. In some places you have 20 centimeters of soil. In some places you have a half meter of soil. In some places you have two meters of soil. The variation depends on the level of soil on the surface, but more or less, all the soils have the same characteristics - a lot of stones coming from the mountains. When the glaciers melted, these big movements of water and stones came down and formed the soils where we now cultivate.

What we are doing is thoroughly studying the characteristics of the different areas and the different soils, and we built a winery that reflects what we have in the vineyard.

How does the chalk manifest itself in the wines? How does this produce a better wine than you get in other regions?

I wouldn't say better, I would say different, because in wine, difference is the important thing. I think chalk gives a special texture in the mouth, a special minerality, but I can say I let you try a stone and you will find in the stone the texture that you will find in the wines after.

Tell us about this beautiful building that you're constructing right now.

It is a new winery. We are very focused on showing in our wines the character of the different regions in the Uco Valley. A few years ago Sebastián, my older son, started working as an agronomist in the company. He was developing all our projects in the Uco Valley. At the same time, he led an area of research on development of the winery. We started a project to build a winery here in the Uco Valley.

Then we started developing a type of vat that is all concrete, and all round. In nature, you will never have square forms. We follow nature. At the same time, we were working in the vineyard to learn about the different terroirs we have, in order to better understand the characteristics of the different types of soils we have. This is a winery where we want to show the real character of the terroir. The real character of this area.

What is your philosophy of winemaking?

From our point of view, the wine is made in the vineyard. What we have to do is show what the vines can produce in this environment, in this area. Then we try to pick the grapes at the right time. Then we separate all the different areas where we produce into smaller sections we call poligons. These areas seem similar, but we explore underground because sometimes all the land looks the same but when you go deeper, you find a lot of differences. You have to think that this area was formed by alluvial movements, very impressive movements where all the stones you can see here are round. They came rolling down from the Andes. At the beginning, it was a totally uneven surface. Then after millions of years, it was filled with thinner soil, because of the wind or the rains or smaller alluvial movements. Then you see the surface and it all looks the same. When you explore and you go deeper, you understand that there are different kinds of soils.

We did a lot of studies and we separated the different areas and we try to pick the grapes in each area at the right time. It is important. We don't want to over-ripen the grapes. We want to keep the character of the vineyard in the wines. Also, we don't like to over-oak. We like to keep the freshness as well as the character of the grapes from the different parts of the vineyard.

Malbec in Argentina has really exploded on the international scene over the last 10 years. The style that most people are familiar with in the US is a bigger, high alcohol Malbec. What I've been seeing here and the wines I've tasted that you made, have much more balance and are much more sophisticated. Tell us about the movement towards balance.

More elegant. My son Sebastián is very oriented in that direction. We think that we are in a place where the weather, with its big variations in temperature between night and day, allows us to ripen the grapes very well. Also, we can achieve a very good level of natural acidity. Then it's interesting to show the character of the region. To have the right ripening. When you over-ripen or when you try to do a big wine, you lose the elegance. We think the freshness, the elegance, is the beauty of a wine. I think in Argentina wine is the national beverage. We celebrate everything. For us, it's part of the food. We never consider wine as alcohol. Wine is food for us. It's part of our culture.

We love to drink a bottle of wine to feel the character of the wine. We like to show the real character coming from the vineyard, as well as the freshness and the elegance. It's very, very important. It's why we are working in that direction. I think it's what is really, in this area in Altamira and in the Uco Valley, possible to produce.

Do you farm sustainably?

In our point of view, it's very, very important to be sustainable. We have internally in the company a program we call "Sustainable by Nature." A big part of our vineyard is organic certified. We are in a region that is very healthy. We don't need to use any artificial products. We can work in a very natural way. Because our soils are very poor in organic material, we do cover our crops during the winter. We have fantastic sunlight in winter, nice temperatures for the barley and vegetables to grow. We then incorporate more organic material in the soil.

Also, we compost and worm compost. We use a compost tea in the irrigation system that incorporates a lot of microorganisms and organic material in the soil. Also, we put compost in the soil. We recycle everything we use. All the water we use in the winery, we recycle. All the skin and stems of the grapes, we compost. We compost and we go back to the vineyard with everything we're taking through the grapes.

Ruta Prov 33 km 7,5, M5531 Maipú, Mendoza, Argentina
+54-261-441000

http://www.familiazuccardi.com

GIRARDO MICHELINI
ZORZAL

During a week long visit to Mendoza we asked many wine people what aspect of Argentine wine they are most excited about. The answer that came back from most was wine coming out of the high altitude Uco Valley sub-region of Gualtallary. When asked who is innovating, the name most often mentioned is the Michelini brothers and their estate, Zorzal.

Zorzal was established in 2007 by founder and general manager Gerardo Michelini, and his winemaking brothers, Juan Pablo and Matías. The estate is located just 80 kilometers southwest of Mendoza, and is situated at 1,350 meters above sea level (the highest of any winery in the region). It is not a place where one would logically think to engage in agriculture.

The Gualtallary terroir is extreme. It is a parched desert-like area with shrubs and cactus blending into a barren landscape. The terroir at Zorzal is derived from a rocky limestone soil, with chalk-streaked stones tempered by a breeze from the Andes. The winery practices organic methods in the vineyards and uses indigenous yeast in the winemaking process.

The Michelinis are making a new style of Malbec - lean, bright and crisp, a radical departure from the big high alcohol Malbecs that put Argentina on the wine map. Zorzal tends to pick its grapes a little earlier (greener) than most in Mendoza to retain freshness and acidity in their wines instead of the overblown ripeness that is too often seen.

Gerardo, you used to be a banker in Mallorca.

Yes. In another life.

In another life. Then, you followed your dream. Most people are too scared to give up their jobs, and the money, go back and do what they really dream about. How did you find the courage to do that?

My education is in finance, originally. The dream I had with my brothers was to build this winery in this place. I worked in a bank to obtain the funding to arrive at this point. Banking was not the end, it was the way. It was the journey to arrive here.

We've been in Mendoza for a few days now, and when we ask what is the future of Mendoza, where are the best wines getting made, pretty much everybody is talking about Gualtallary, which is where we are right now. Tell us about how you found this spot, and what the terroir means to you.

Terroir is everything for me, for the winery. We imagine this place in different ways. First the soil, we have unique soil in Argentina. It's almost 100% calcareous or "calcareo" in Spanish. It's not usual in Argentina. This is the first thing, because calcareous soil gives the wine an austerity, a minerality that is not usual in Argentina. Argentina normally makes a huge Malbec, sweet Malbecs, but this calcareous gives the wine minerality, austerity and terroir.

We've talked to a number of winemakers that have talked about modern winemaking in Argentina. In most Old World

23

countries, modern winemaking means higher alcohol, bigger wines, more fruit. Here it's the other way around. Modern is going back to what is happening in the Old World and making leaner, lower alcohol, higher acid wines.

In Argentina, we have a different conception. For us, traditional wines are the kind that Argentina used to make, big Malbecs with body, jammy. For us, the modern wines are light, elegant, with acidity, easy to drink, easy to pair with food. We imagine more wines like this, but you have a reason. We are looking to Europe, the north of France, the Loire, Burgundy. These regions are for me, the best regions to make good wines.

Tell us about the wines that you are making right now.

We make wines like this. Wines that are fresh because we are in the fresh region of Mendoza. The altitude is at 1,400 meters high. As a result, the wines will be fresh. We are in the desert, like Mexico. Therefore, the wines are mineral, not jammy.

Gerardo, you started in 2008, is that correct? How has the winemaking evolved since you began making wine here?

We change everyday, everyday. When I think about when we started in 2008 and I see where we are today, we changed everything. We started with these traditional wines and wines with more body, but we learned that this place is different and we changed year by year to more wild wines than the wines we made in the past.

You mention wild wines, what does that mean to you? What does it mean to make a wild wine?

Wild wine is not wine with sugar, not sugar wines, but wines dry like arrows. Dirt wines get inside you. This is wild like an arrow.

Is it picking early?

The most important change is that we do nothing. We try to do nothing. We leave the grapes, 80% with the complete bunch, and wait. We just wait for the natural gift of this place. It's just the easiest way to make wine. We do nothing, we only wait, but we have an amazing valley with very healthy grapes and intervention would do bad things. Don't intervene with the wines.

Tell us about your agricultural practices. How do you go about growing your grapes?

In the vineyard, we farm organically and we are starting with the newest biodynamic process, which is not usual in Argentina. We started with biodynamics two years ago and we are falling in love with this process.

Do you have a favorite wine region?

I love the Loire. I love Sancerre. I love Agneau, but I love my wines too.

Gerardo, you do something very interesting with the way you vinify your wines. Tell us about that process.

We work with egg-shaped vats that we love because they are different than the barrels. They are similar in shape, but the eggs don't put wood notes in the wine. That is a big challenge for us because when we saw eggs in France, we asked for these eggs to bring to Argentina and the price was huge. We decided to copy them using pictures and we developed them here in Argentina and it was much cheaper than buying them in France.

We started with one egg in 2011 and now we have about 20. In Argentina, there are now a lot of wineries with eggs. They copied us.

I've seen a few.

It was our idea. We didn't patent them. We didn't register the idea

25

and the constructor earned a lot of money from our idea. The shape is very nice for completing the wine because the juices inside are in permanent movement, and convection movement gives the wine more complexity and more body.

How much wine are you making at the moment?

We make around 500,000 bottles per year.

That's quite a bit to be doing after such a short period of time.

Well, we grow every year. A lot of people worldwide want to see what we are doing here. This is fantastic for us, for our philosophy.

Zorzal was a dream for us. For me and my brothers. Every time we imagined a winery, we imagined it here in this place. We all worked in different wineries, as employees. We always dreamed of building a home here place in Mendoza, in Gualtallary. One day we did it and we are here.

Gerardo, tell us why you decided to get into the wine business?

This is a family tradition. My grandparents were born in Italy. Our last name is Michelini, we are from the north of Italy. They came to Argentina as immigrants. They decided to start here in Mendoza because they wanted to make wine.

We love the terroir. We love the soil, the sun, the climate. Our philosophy is to make wine, to represent the terroir, this place.

What does Zorzal mean?

Zorzal is a bird. A very ugly bird, but with a very beautiful song. We have a very famous tango singer who we call the Zorzal for his song. Zorzal in Argentina means tango, it means passion!

Camino Estancia Silva s/n - Tupungato, Mendoza , 5561, Argentina
+54 0261-4245249

http://www.zorzalwines.com

PAUL HOBBS
LOS CABOS & FORMER
CONSULTANT AT CATENA ZAPATA

Paul Hobbs' numerous achievements include helping to establish Malbec as the grape of Argentina, founding his own winery and being twice named Wine Personality of the Year by Robert Parker, Jr.

Dorothy J. Gaiter talks to Hobbs about his journey in wine.

Dorothy J. Gaiter: You fell in love with Argentina in 1988?

Paul Hobbs: Yes, but it was only by a sort of a serendipitous event. I went to Chile, not Argentina in March 1988, because I was looking for new challenges in my career. At that time, I was winemaker at Simi Winery in Healdsburg, California. I contacted a classmate friend of mine from U.C. Davis, Marcelo Kogan. Marcelo, at the time was professor of, of all things, weeds.

Weeds?

At the Catholic University in Santiago, Chile. He was also the wine aficionado and he had many contacts with the wineries because they used his knowledge to help manage, I guess, weeds. He invited me and organized all my visits for a week in Chile. I invited another classmate friend, Jorge Catena.

I know that name.

Nicolás' younger brother, also a classmate. Jorge drove over the Andes to be with us. I did not realize that there was a problem between the Chileans and the Argentines and so when Jorge showed up, that immediately created a problem for Marcelo.

Marcelo asked me first where he was from and I told him Argentina, so that put a very furrowed look on his face. Then, after that, he asked me, what does he do and I said, "Well, he's a winemaker." He thought

not only have you invited our enemy, but you've invited a spy as well.

I told Jorge you have to go back, but Jorge wouldn't go back. I said, "Our host is not very happy with your being here." This was the time of Pinochet and the Falkland Islands, the Malvinas as they prefer to call them in Argentina.

Right.

I was unaware of the history and the problem that Jorge's visit had created. Kogan forbade me to take Catena on any trip or any visit. Then, Catena wouldn't return to Argentina. He stayed there the entire week. Finally, on Thursday afternoon, I decided, "Well, there's no real secrets that I can see here."

Jorge invited me to lunch, so I decided well... I got a little drunk, maybe. No, not really, but I drank a little wine and decided well, I'll take him on a visit. When I got home to Marcelo's place that night, my luggage was outside his door. That's how I got to Argentina.

We drove over the Andes on Friday morning and I met his brother Nicolás that began our association for nine years.

Now, they wanted to talk to you about Chardonnay, right?

Oddly, today anybody would consider that to be an odd idea.

Nicolás had one thought and that was that Chardonnay would prove to the world that Argentina could make world class wines because he reasoned that white wines were more technically challenging to make than reds. It would require more technology. So if we could make a high-quality white, then he reasoned that they would accept the reds automatically out of hand.

How did you shift that to Malbec?

That was actually another little issue that occurred because Nicolás did not want to make Malbec, but our importer wanted a red wine. Of course, the logical red wine was to make Cabernet Sauvignon. Nicolás had a vineyard, so ... I, however, became infatuated with the Malbec grape, something I didn't know or had familiarity with.

Nicolás Catena had an old vineyard, nearly a 100-year-old vineyard in a little area called Lunlunta along the Rio Mendoza river. That old vineyard inspired me and so even against Nicolás' wishes, because I asked Nicolás if he would help finance some experimental trials with the grape, I proceeded.

He said, "No, the French have already demonstrated. They did not replant after phylloxera. They have already demonstrated as well, documented in the literature about this grape, so we're not going to invest in Malbec." Nevertheless, his head viticulturist humored me and we began working on a section of the vineyard to grow the grapes in a way that I needed them grown.

Then, I was able to get 10 free American oak barrels. I grabbed these from a gentleman by the name of Alain Fouquet who was the head of Seguin Moreau, the famous Tonnellerie in Cognac, France. He gave me the 10 barrels of American oak because he wanted to build a Tonnellerie or a cooperage in Napa.

Today it's called Napa Cooperage.

That's his business?

He started that. These barrels that he sent to Argentina helped in demonstrating that that was possible because I made the first Malbecs in those barrels. When we did a tasting of wines in March 1993 for the American press, the show to launch the Chardonnay from Catena, that was the opportunity that I took to show them the Malbec.

Thomas Stockley, the writer for the *Seattle Times*, wrote an article after that tasting called, "Don't cry for me Argentina," and he largely talked about the Malbec and the guests indicated that they liked it. Nicolás decided in this case, we should make Malbec, and so he changed. That was the beginning of a brand that is well-known today called Alamos.

What's your general philosophy of winemaking? You've been at it for a long time, and you're really great at it. What are your thoughts on how you do it and why you do it?

Philosophically, from my perception, wine's about enjoyment, but it's also, in addition to that, wine ties us back to some place. Some people call it a somewhereness, some people call it terroir. There are many different ways of looking at it, but that's always been important to me. My father was the first to introduce the concept to me, I think. Growing up on a fruit farm, we had six or seven individual (mostly apples), apple farms in upstate New York, in Niagara County. My father enjoyed putting me to the blind tasting of matching apples to the farm. He'd take a Macintosh, for example, and he loved to line up all the Macintosh from each of the farms, blind, and ask me to discern which was which.

That was a challenge, but you know it's funny, because even the color varied. The crispness, some element of the flavor would vary, and finally if you studied it carefully, my father said you'll begin to see those differences. That has always been with me. Also I've been inspired by others. During the time that I worked with Robert Mondavi - and I was on the first Opus One team - I learned that as well. Also the French have been very instrumental in my appreciation of a sense of place. When I started Paul Hobbs Winery, that was the most important aspect, how to achieve a true sense of place. That's what I've found means a minimalistic approach to winemaking, and, maybe even more importantly, to farming.

It goes well beyond organic where it's just simply the use of organic practices, or organic pesticides, this kind of thing. It's really a whole concept of how to farm a vineyard in a way that, let's say, nurtures the fruit and the vine in a very natural way. There are a lot of elements to that, so rather than go into all of that, let's just say that it's gratifying. There's been an important evolution and even a revolution in some sense, in the sense of the farming. We have to do that, because I also choose to ferment only with indigenous yeast from the bloom, or the grapes that we harvest. By using pesticide, or particularly any harsh pesticide, that would damage the indigenous yeasts. We would kill them, and they would not be able to conduct fermentation in which case that process wouldn't really work out, would it?

This is serious sustainability.

This is serious sustainability, and that's in fact the word that I like, it's sustainable farming. We try to work as much as possible in that way. In the winery, in essence, we have very simple wineries, and cleanliness in this case I have found to be one of the most important factors to managing quality, because we eschew any practices like filtration or refining that could alter the character of the wine. We don't use any filtration centrifugation. We do not add any kind of element at all to the wine, except maybe from time to time we may correct the acidity with tartaric acid, or we may add a small amount of sulfur dioxide.

We have very, very, low addition of S02 as well to our wines. We have found many practices, and this has been a lifelong work. It's a passion of mine particularly since I was able to work under my own label. That's the driving philosophy.

That's pretty awesome and holistic. There's been criticism of winemakers who chase scores, high scores, and a lot of debate about Parker's influence, that wines that tend to be huge and over-extracted get his attention. What do you think about that, and what is it that you're trying to do?

Well, Mr. Parker, as we all know, has become the most influential critic not only for wine, but of any type of subject matter, whether it be art … He became the most influential critic of all time, the world has ever known. I don't think it'll ever happen again.

With that kind of power, is the ability to influence buyers, and buyers with money. If you've got a big score, wineries begin to chase scores, because that meant you put your wines in the hands of where you wanted your wines and you could charge more. Every winery wants to optimize their profit, as does anyone in business. That led to, I think, a misunderstanding, and I don't think that was ever intended. It was a disservice to Mr. Parker's work. My feeling is that Robert Parker, number one, is a brilliant taster and one of the most enjoyable people on the planet to be with. His personality, I think, came through in his writing, and that was a huge attraction to people when he was really truly enthusiastic about a wine.

Passionate.

Passionate. With a capital P. I found him to be not interested in over-extracted wines as much as I think people talk. He was more balanced. I think there was a misconception, and I think many people really didn't understand how to get where he wanted probably to see some people go. I felt, for example, everybody thought I would say, or many people thought that they should ripen the grapes to a very high sugar level. That wasn't really the idea at all. It wasn't about the sugar, it was about getting the phenolics and the physiology of the plant fully ripe, the seeds ripe, so the tannins would be sweet.

They misunderstood that.

I think there were a lot of misunderstandings, finally, and so I think it went a little bit caddywhompus. It got out of control. I think everybody was influenced, to some degree, and I will include myself. It's hard not to be, and the '90s were so super heated. The economy was crazy, everything was crazy, so it just got all out of kilter, I'd say.

Now the pendulum seems to be swinging back to elegance, and finesse, and balance. I read a lot about balance.

Balance is back.

Finesse and elegance were almost dirty words, because it sort of implied wimpy, or weak. Now everybody's okay to say those words again, meaning finesse means sophistication, elegance, layers. It's more like, I don't know, for a guy that likes automobiles, it's more like power and complexity and elegance all in a balanced packaged. More like what you would find in a fine Porsche, for example, versus maybe a Corvette. I don't know, I haven't driven a Corvette in a long time, but I had one, and it was all about power. I had one when I was a kid.

Costa Flores and Route 7, Perdriel,
Lujan de Cuyo, Mendoza

http://www.vinacobos.com

JOSÉ GALANTE
SALENTEIN

José Galante was one of Argentina's Malbec pioneers. He worked at Catena Zapata for 34 years before leaving for Bodegas Salentein. Working alongside consultant Paul Hobbs and viticulturist Pedro Marchevsky, he is one of the key figures in Catena Zapata's huge international success and of the explosion of Malbec.

Galante left Catena for Dutch-owned Salentein which sits 1,500 meters above sea level in the Uco Valley and produces cool climate Malbec, Pinot Noir, Chardonnay and Sauvignon Blanc. Some of Salentein's vineyards can be traced back to the Jesuits of the 17th century.

Galante also has his own personal project and makes wine for Huentala wines in Gualtallary in the Uco Valley.

The text below consists of two interviews - first with José Galante talking to Dorothy J. Gaiter in New York City about the Uco Valley and how the Argentine economy impacts its wine trade. The second took place in Huentala Wines in Mendoza.

You make wine in the Uco Valley, in Argentina.

Yes. 100% of our vineyard is located in Uco Valley.

Uco Valley is a beautiful region in the west of Mendoza. It was the last region developed in Argentina, and began to produce high-quality wines in the last 20 years when grape irrigation arrived in Argentina. That was the main reason to develop this area. It's a beautiful area

34

because it's in the slope of the mountain.

That sounds beautiful.

The climatic condition, the possibility of producing grapes at different altitudes with different flavors, different air pressure, I think is the most attractive aspect for us. Especially in Salentein, because Salentein has 2,000 hectares, with vineyards on more than 800 hectares. Our vineyards go from 1,000 meters to 1,700 meters.

So you have a lot of different microclimates to work with.

Yes. This is very difficult to explain because in a short distance, only 22 kilometers, the ripeness of the grape can be different. And the expression of the grape also is different from one place to another.

Must be very fun for a winemaker though, right?

Yes. For example: Chardonnay. We have Chardonnay at three different altitudes. And the Chardonnay at the low altitude usually has more tropical flavor.

But in the middle is more pears, apple, this kind of flavor. In the higher altitude, there's the most exciting Chardonnay with citrus, a lot of minerals, good flavor, good acidity.

At the highest altitude?

In the high altitude, the same with the Malbec, the same with the Pinot Noir. Also, it's different, the timing of the moment of picking the grape. For example, in the low altitude, we pick Chardonnay at the beginning of March. In the high altitude, we pick at the end of April, more than one month later.

It's all handpicked as well, right?

Yes. All our grapes are picked by hand. Our winery is in the middle of the vineyard. Just a few minutes after we pick the grapes, we have the grapes in our winery and we have control of the different situations.

Okay. You are well-known for helping introduce Malbec to Americans. Was it difficult to sell Malbec to Americans in the beginning? You worked for Catena Zapata for 34 years?

At the beginning, our expectation with Malbec was not too strong, not very confident. Nothing like the success we have now with Malbec. It was a new flavor. But when people tasted Malbec, they fell in love with Malbec. The color is very attractive, the flavor is black fruit, full of flavor, and I think the most exciting feature is the sweetness of the tannins. Malbec is easy to combine with different food. You can drink Malbec with pasta ...

I like it with roast meats. I love meat.

Yes, with everything. I think this is one of the reasons that Malbec is very successful. Also, Malbec is the most important variety. Almost 50% of our portfolio is Malbec. We are working a lot trying to even define the best region to produce Malbec in our vineyard. We are working a lot in two different ways.

One of them is to explore some specific site where we can find the most exciting expression of Malbec. The other way is to explore Malbec blending with another variety. I think these two ways are the future for Malbec in Argentina.

You're a real student. You're an academic student and a

teacher of winemaking? I read that you got your degree at the Universidad Maza. You used to teach there, too?

I taught there for 15 years.

Really?

I no longer am teaching there. I'm more focused now on the winery. I think it was a good experience because it was an opportunity to translate all the information about our beautiful treasures in Argentina.

This Bodegas Salentein, they've got three vineyards, right?

We have three different estates. The higher estate, we call San Paulo. It's a beautiful region in this area.

Sometimes, you have snow in August in that vineyard?

Yes.

That's amazing. That's really high altitude?

Very high altitude. In this area, we produce Chardonnay, Pinot Noir, Sauvignon Blanc, Pinot Meunier also. In the middle we produce a lot of Chardonnay, Pinot Noir, Sauvignon Blanc. We are now planting more Malbec, and a little Merlot. The low altitude, we say low altitude, but this is 1,200 meters high. For us it is low altitude, but not for other makers of wine. In this area, we have Cabernet Sauvignon, Cabernet Franc, Merlot, Tempranillo, a lot of different varieties.

When people think of Argentine wines, they think of Malbec. Are there other varietals that you're very excited about?

We have a lot of different varietals. I think one of the varietals that could be successful in the future is Cabernet Franc because the expression and the flavor of the Cabernet Franc in our region are so nice. I love Cabernet Sauvignon. I love Chardonnay. I love Pinot Noir. We are producing, I think, good references of these wines.

I love Cabernet Franc. Why is it doing so well there?

I think because of our climatic conditions, Cabernet Franc grows very well and it's sweet, round, and has a lot of flavor. There is a lot of potential in Cabernet Franc. I think Cabernet Franc is a varietal that is not too strong. It's clean and here we can produce a good expression of the varietal. Our Cabernet Franc, we began to produce and now it's very successful in our portfolio.

Your winery is owned by a Dutch company and that's where it

got its name, right? This is the name of a 17th century castle, right?

Yes, it's the castle. It's a beautiful castle and it's the name of our wine, yes.

The current winery is some spectacular destination winery, I've read. You've got a resort, you've got a gallery, you've got restaurants, you've got this amazing wine facility.

I think Mr. Pon was very visionary when he decided to invest in the Uco Valley because he bought the best land and he helped the region develop. He was a real pioneer to start. After, then to start planting vineyards at 5,400 feet, creating an art gallery there, a hot spot of tourism.

Yes, yes. Imagine when Mr. Pon arrived in the Uco Valley, there was nothing in this area. It had only the natural vegetation. Imagine our average rain in this area is 200 millimeters. It's a desert. He decided at the beginning to buy this land. Then, he decided to plant his vineyard and to build a beautiful restaurant, art gallery, and of course, a wonderful winery with all the new technology.

I think it was a tremendous decision because I remember hearing that everybody thought, "This man is crazy." There was no other investment in the area for a long time. Mr. Pon was a real visionary to develop Uco Valley.

That's incredible to have that kind of foresight. With Argentina's economy going through a difficult time now, is that having an effect on the way you can sell the wine, the prices that you can ask for? Is it affecting your ability to sell your wine?

We're very optimistic about the future because usually Argentina goes up and down, up and down. I think in a few months we will see improvements in the economy. We are continuing with our project. I think the most important thing for us is that 100% of our grapes are produced in our vineyards. We have all the control in all the different stages of production. This is one of the reasons we are very optimistic.

Okay. The Netherlands and Argentina have become very close in recent years. The queen of the Netherlands is from Argentina. Have your wines been served at any of the official affairs, any big parties, weddings?

Maxima and Willem-Alexander were married in 2002 and Pinot Noir was served, our Pinot Noir.

Is that right? The Pinot Noir? Not the Malbec? That's interesting.

It was Pinot Noir. Now, in the future, we would serve Malbec.

That's wonderful. She became queen last year.

Yes. For us, it's a very big honor. Maxima is a lady. For us, it's very important to know that she is the queen and also represents our country.

Is the Netherlands a big market for your wines?

Yes. In Europe the main market is the Netherlands, yes.

If you could describe your wines with one word, what one word would you use?

Now, I feel very happy because people in the world are changing their ideas about wine. A few years ago, people complained that wines were "too strong, too concentrated." Now, people like a wine that you can drink with food. People prefer a wine with more elegance, with finesse. This is the wine that we are producing in our winery. We're always thinking of the consumer. If people drink a bottle of wine and it's good, they'll think 'I'd like to drink another.'

Interview with Christopher Barnes

You have been a winemaker at Catena for 34 years, and you've been a winemaker at Salentein for five years. There are probably very few people in Mendoza who know the terroir as well as you do. Tell us a little bit about Gualtallary, and the importance of Gualtallary in the terroir of modern Mendoza winemaking.

Well, Gualtallary is a beautiful area because it's in a high altitude, and as a result the quality of the grapes are much better to produce wines in the modern style. This is important because you have in the grape a very nice relationship between the sugar, the acidity, and the pH. This is very important because when you have a good balance between acidity, alcohol, and the pH, you have good balance in your mouth. Less alcohol, more fruit, and good freshness at the end, in relation with the acidity and the pH.

I think this area is very nice for all these reasons, and in the end, it means good acidity, good freshness, less alcohol. Wine marked with more elegance, more finesse, more balance.

How did the transition occur from traditional winemaking of Mendoza to this new modern style?

A few years ago, people liked to produce wine with high alcohol concentration, a lot of oak, and with tannin structure. But I don't think this style of wine is good to drink for lunch or dinner.

This wine is very difficult to drink. People today prefer more friendly wines. Wine that you enjoy drinking a glass, and then another, and finally the bottle. I always try to produce a wine with elegance and finesse. I never like to produce wine with a style that is too strong, too heavy, and too difficult to drink.

Terrific. Tell us about the terroir of Gualtallary. What is unique about the soil composition and the climate here that makes the wine so interesting?

This soil is different compared to other areas in the Uco Valley. Here you have a sandy soil with stone, but also in one meter there is some calcarea, and you can taste the flavor in the grapes. Usually in this area you have thicker skin, and when you taste the grapes you can always taste some minerality. In my perception, I describe this minerality like a graphite. "Grafito" in Spanish. I don't know the word in English, but this kind of aroma. This kind of flavor, and this is exciting because it's difficult to find this aroma, this flavor in Malbec. Also in this area we have good spicy flavor, flora flavor. It's nice because when you taste Malbec from other regions in the Uco Valley, you can always identify the grapes from Gualtallary.

You have a couple of personal projects that you're working on at the moment. Perhaps you can start by telling us about Huentala, and how you got involved with it, and how the project has evolved.

The owner of Huentala is a close friend, and I help Julio to produce his wines. I like working with Julio because he's nice, and he has a lot of passion. He lives life with a lot of intensity. In my personal project, I made wine from different areas in Mendoza, and I selected the Uco Valley because I think it's the best wine-producing area. My philosophy here is to use grapes from different areas and blend a Malbec to represent the different area of the Uco Valley. Huentala is 100% Gualtallary.

Having been part of some of the most important and iconic wineries in Argentina, what is it like being an entrepreneur and starting your own label?

It's a family project. I work with my wife, my son and my daughter and it's nice because we do everything in relation to the wine. We select the grapes, we work together during the winemaking, and it's nice because what you have is a perfect combination, passion for wine and the love of family. It's nice because when you put it all together it's very strong, and you live with a lot of passion, and a lot of energy.

Perhaps you can talk about Huentala, when it started, and how it has evolved, in terms of planting the grapes and making the first wines.

The first production was in 2012. In 2013 we produced the first wine with the Huentala label. The idea is to grow, but always think in terms of a high-quality label, with good quality wine. Yes. I think this area is only for producing high-quality wine, not average wine.

It's very interesting that it's a very young area, and it is so tremendously hot right now. Everybody is talking about it. In a lot of older regions that have been making wine for longer periods of time, everybody talks about old vines. Here this region is producing such interesting terroir and the young vines seen to be something that everyone is excited about.

Yes. Yes. For me, it's exciting to think of the future and what will happen with this grape when it is 20, 30 years old. Maybe the quality will be amazing because now the young plant produces a very nice quality of grape, imagine what could happen in 10 or 15 years. In the future, I think this area could be fantastic.

I understand there's an interesting program with Huentala wines involving some of the top winemakers in Mendoza.

Yes. Yes. Yes. The idea is to take the grapes from this vineyard and have different winemakers produce wine. For example, in 2015, the people involved who produced wines were Marcelo Paradiso and Roberto de la Motta. In talking with Julio, I said, "Imagine when we have a vertical tasting with the same grapes, but with different winemakers. How very exciting it would be when we have the opportunity to have the vertical tasting."

That's very interesting. Red Hook Winery in New York does something similar. They take grapes from the same plot, and they give them to two very different wineries. Robert Foley, who's very traditional Napa, and Abe Schoener who's the crazy man of Napa, who does very experimental winemaking. You see how the two wines are very, very different even though they're the same core grapes.

Yes. I have the opportunity to taste wine from the different

41

winemakers, and you taste the difference...

Fingerprints?

Yes. Yes. It's difficult for me to explain in English, but all the different winemakers have the same ideas, and they have different ideas, and when you taste the wine you feel the difference. For me I enjoy it a lot because it's nice to taste the wines. Yes, to taste the differences.

Bodegas Salentein
Ruta 89 s/n. Km 14. Localidad de Los Árboles. Departamento de Tunuyán
+54 0261 4311698

http://www.bodegasalentein.com/

Huentala Wines
Stay Way Silva S/N M5561BTA
Gualtallary, Tupungato, Mendoza
+54 261 4200766

http://huentalawines.com

MENDOZA, ARGENTINA

DANIEL PI
TRAPICHE

Trapiche is one of Argentina's oldest wineries. It was established in 1883 at the foothills of the Andes in Mendoza. It is the largest exporter of Argentine wine by volume and is in over 80 markets. Led by winemaker Daniel Pi, Trapiche sources grapes from Argentina's best winegrowing sites, including more than 2,400 acres of proprietary vineyards and a stable of more than 200 independent growers.

There are few wineries out there producing wine at an $8 price that can compare to the quality of Trapiche. And with their single vineyard Icsay, Finca Las Palmas and Gran Medalla series, they are also making interesting wines at the higher end. We talk to winemaker Daniel Pi about making value wines and the history of Argentine Malbec in Argentina.

Daniel, tell us about Trapiche.

Trapiche was founded in 1883. It's one of the oldest continuously running wineries in Argentina. When it was founded, the Argentine wine industry was very robust due to the establishment of a railway line to Mendoza. Many immigrants arrived from Spain and Italy. Some came from France as well. That was the beginning of the wine industry in Argentina. We became one of the biggest wine producers in the world. Actually, Argentina is the fifth largest wine producer in the world.

Wow.

Also, we are one of the best wine drinkers in the world. That's why Argentina is so well-known in the world today...because of Malbec. Malbec came from very old vines in Argentina. The industry began

more than 130 years ago.

Has Malbec always been an important grape for Trapiche? Or is it something more recent, since the explosion of Malbec on the international scene in the last 20 years?

Malbec was our main grape variety for many years. The main reason was at that time the government rulers decided to give a boost to the wine industry and they hired French viticulturists. One of them was the youthful agronomist, Miguel Pouget, who was highly influential in developing the wine industry in Mendoza. He thought that the best wines came from Bordeaux and he imported the first French Malbec varietals. All the pre-phylloxera Bordeaux blends were made basically with Malbec. In Bordeaux Malbec was very important. After phylloxera, it wasn't as important as it is today.

Merlot took the place of Malbec. For us it was very important because we took all the vines, all the shoots from Bordeaux cuttings at that time. We replicated what those viticulturists did 130,140 years ago. Malbec was important. Cabernet Sauvignon was important. There was some Petit Verdot as well that we can find in the oldest vineyards here in Mendoza. We had the good fortune not to get any of the diseases that attacked Europe in those days. We survived, and we kept the original DNA material from Bordeaux from many, many years ago.

This was something that we found out 20 years ago when we had to

45

plant more and more Malbec. We did it in another way because we used to have flood irrigation or furrow irrigation. All the consultants said if we go into drip irrigation we would have some problems, or if we go with unrooted vines which was very popular in Argentina that time. We had to graft vines onto American root stalks. I said, "Why can't we buy the ripe Malbec from France?" We imported vines from France at that time, 20 years ago. After five years, we said okay, but this is not our Malbec. This is something different, because it's big clusters, big berries. It's not the same as we have, small clusters, small berries. The shape of the leaves is the same, but the clonal selection that the people in France made was based on productivity instead of quality. We didn't get the right quality from those grapes.

At that time 20 years ago, we tried to replicate our old material, grafting on American root stalks as well. Instead of having clonal we, at Trapiche at least, wanted to have some other selections. Some from populations of high-quality vineyards. We replicated those vineyard selections that we made on our own. We kept all the old vines that we got from France at that time. We called it the synonym of Malbec, which is Côt. We used the term Côt in Mendoza for the French clones that we imported during the 1990s. For the material that we got from the original vines from 130,140 years ago, we called Malbec. That makes our Malbec unique compared with other Malbecs that you find in other areas.

How old are some of your vines? And, were you able to keep a lot of the original vines?

We have some of our old vines that we call the first growing area. Trapiche is located in the surroundings of Maipú and Luján. It's the place that is known as the first growing area, because it was the first place the immigrants settled their vineyards. The main reason why we are here is irrigation. We have the channels of water melting from the Mendoza River in the Andes Mountains. All the water comes into the Luján de Cuyo area. There is a dam there for all the channels of irrigation. So one of the reasons is water. We have water availability.

The other reason the immigrants settled the vineyards here is because we are quite close to the city. The main reason, as I explained, is the railway. We are near the main railway that goes from Santiago de Chile to Buenos Aires, which is called the Buenos Aires to the Pacific Railway. Before the railway, the only way at that time to reach Buenos Aires - which is the main city of Argentina, where half of the population lives and drinks wine - was by big cars pulled by bulls. It took about two months. From Mendoza, it was 1100 kilometers to Buenos Aires. At that time the population of Buenos Aires drank

French wine, because it was cheaper and in some ways better as there was some spoilage from the Mendoza wine traveling two months in very bad conditions.

At that time, people in Buenos Aires also used to drink more French wine because we shipped beef to Europe as well as some grains, like wheat and all those commodities from the Pampas. From Europe to Buenos Aires you have to ship something back. There were many Bordeaux wines coming here. Mostly we were drinking Claret. When our wine industry got a boost, and the railway arrived, it only took two days to get to Buenos Aires. Sorry France, but we started to drink our own wines. The quality was very good. We were happy. There were a lot of immigrants coming from the Mediterranean countries. Spain, as I told you. France, Italy. They know how to drink wine. They used to drink a lot.

With the old vines that you still have, can you tell the difference between the wines that are made from those plots

and the wines that are made from the more recently planted plots?

Yes. Old vines are like old guys. They don't produce a lot of fruit. They have been producing a lot of fruit during their lifetime. The small quantity of fruit the old vines yield is perfect in quality and balance within the capacity of the vines. We have vineyards that are over 60 years old still running, especially in the Mendoza bed of the Mendoza River. They are mostly Cabernet Sauvignon and Malbec. I love them because those old vines have very deep root systems of more than three meters. They are about 10 feet deep. They are in good shape and they produce less than one bottle per vine, in very nice equilibrium and concentration.

Compared with young vines less than 20 years old, we have vines that we usually have to trim. You have to trellis them. You have to educate, in some way, in order to produce good quality. They can produce, and they do produce, very good quality. It's like when you are young. You make a lot of mistakes if you don't have some education. It's the same with old and young vines. We are lucky to have these old vines. The problem is, most of these old vines are located in this area where we have transportation and water, but not the climate. Most of the young vines are located in better growing conditions for high quality. That means that we are more on the slopes of the Andes. A little bit south and west in the Uco Valley. Most of the good quality Malbecs and Cabernet Sauvignon today come from the Uco Valley, where there are younger vines and very high-quality vineyards. The old vines are located in this surrounding area, which are also producing very good quality wines as well.

Tell us about your philosophy of winemaking, Daniel.

It has been changing. I have been a winemaker for the last 30 years. At the beginning, the wine industry was more dedicated to making wine in the style that the market required. It always was the same. If I had to review my life as a winemaker, my philosophy is more consumer orientated. The tastes of the consumer have been changing. Demand also has changed in the last 30 years. I remember when I started, white wine was more popular than red. Today it is the opposite. My main objective, always, is to respect the consumer. To produce a proper quality and price relationship. I think this is also something that Trapiche agrees with. For us the main target for our design of the wines is respect and value. I think that is something people know about at Trapiche. Every time people open a bottle of Trapiche they know the value of the wine that they are drinking. It's amazing. This is our philosophy.

48

Obviously, when we go up in the pyramid of our portfolio and we are up to the very top end, these wines, which is, for us, like the Formula One wines, we try to show what Argentina can produce in terms of outstanding quality. The value is the terroir, the place where the grapes come from. We are not trying to manipulate them in any way. We are trying to give more respect, in this case, to the place where the grapes come from, in order to communicate the value of Argentine wine. This is more or less my philosophy and the Trapiche philosophy as well.

Are there other regions or other winemakers that have influenced you in terms of the styles of your wines?

In the beginning I studied in Mendoza. At that time, it was the only university in South America or Latin America in general, where one could become a winemaker. There were a lot of self-made

49

winemakers that taught us. It wasn't very easy 30 years ago to travel and to have experiences in other places. Everything was communicated by these self-taught winemakers and magazines and books. Today, everything is easier. We have the internet. We know immediately what is happening. We have better communications.

Then I had the opportunity to go abroad and make wine. I mainly worked in North America - in Washington State and California. I learned more about the wine industry in a young country such as the US. The value and the respect that the consumer in the US was getting in the wines and the revolution that occurred in those days, in the early 1980s, was impressive. It was something we winemakers always dreamed about in Argentina; to reach this point of recognition that the wines in North America had.

During the 1990s we had the opportunity to interact with some flying winemakers. I had a chance to work with Michel Roland. Today we are working with Alberto Antonini. There were a lot of investors in Mendoza from Italy, France, and from Europe in general. Also people from the US. We are always learning. We are always open-minded. The wine industry in Argentina is well-known because we share everything among the winemakers. Because we want to take the wine industry, in a short period of time, to the next level.

Today we can truly say that Argentina has made it in a very short period of time. It's well-known for its quality wines. I think it's because we have a mixture of influences. I think in the beginning a lot of influences came from the flying winemakers. Today we are confident. I think we don't need them anymore. In some way we've grown up. We know better than anyone the capabilities of our place, and how to make great wine. Today, I think, we have our own DNA. We practically don't need them. We share a lot of wine with them, of course.

Tell us a bit about your terroir. You have multiple growing zones. You've mentioned that you've focused more on your high-quality wines in the Uco Valley and your value wines are on the Uco Valley floor. Is that correct?

Yes, that is correct in general. Again, going back 20 years ago, we said okay, Mendoza is the place. Depending on the year, 70 to 75% of all the wine in Argentina is produced in Mendoza. San Juan is the second largest growing area, going up the western side of the Andes of Argentina. We have Catamarca and the Calchaquí Valley and also Patagonia, but Mendoza is still the most important place. Over a period of time, we were focusing, we were zooming, finding out which are the best places for growing grapes. We moved up in the Andes for quality. Today we are in some places that also produce high-yield vines, specifically in the floor of the Uco Valley. We have a very nice map that I can show you.

The floor of the Uco Valley, say 650 meters to 758 meters high, is where we have a lot of sun. We have deep soil and enough water to cultivate vines and get high yields. For value wines it is very important. Then we move to the first growing area which is 850 to almost 1000 meters. In Luján and Maipú we get the old vine quality and very nice, supple Malbecs and intense Cabernet Sauvignon from the river bed of the Mendoza River.

The area of the Uco Valley, in the southwest of the first growing area, where we have Tupungato, Tunuyán, and San Carlos, that area 30 years ago was a place mainly dedicated for fruit and some grapes as well. It produced high-color red wines with good acidity to blend with the valley floor grapes, which are lower color and lower acidity, to get some good blending components. Today we are going farther west and drilling wells in order to get the underground water. We have started to explore areas we call border places for growing grapes. We are getting very outstanding quality. This area, which has state-of-the-art new vineyards with very appropriate use of water, very high-quality,

51

high-tech vineyards, is today the best place for me to showcase the potential of Argentina.

How big is Trapiche in terms of how much wine you are making right now? Is this something that has dramatically changed over the last 20 years?

We can say that we were always the first export winery. We started exporting about 100 years ago. In some way, we got a boost during the '70s, but always in terms of simple wines. In the beginning of the 2000s, say 10 to 15 years ago, Trapiche was a million case operation in which 800,000 cases were dedicated to the domestic market and 200,000 for export.

I've been a winemaker for Trapiche since 2003. Today, at Trapiche after 12 years, we are a three million case operation. We have multiplied by three from where we were. We are half domestic and half export today. It's 1.5 million domestic and 1.5 million cases for export. Also, the quality has been growing. We made a dramatic change at Trapiche in terms of quality and volume. It was a very good challenge for winemakers and for growers. We work with a lot of growers, viticulturists, and engineers in order to expand quality. I think we are in that process. Still we are growing much more with our wines of high value, which is, as they say in America, "the sweet spot,"or something like that. I learned that! Which is something like $15 to $20 retail. We are offering, I think, good value for the money. This price point is Trapiche's core business in America and in Argentina as well.

Nueva Mayorga s/n | Entre calles Roca y Mitre Coquimbito Maipu, Mendoza 5521, Argentina
+54 261 5207666

http://www.trapichewines-usa.com

ERNESTO BAJDA
CATENA ZAPATA

Nicolás Catena is described as "the undisputed patriarch of Argentinean fine wine" in Evan Goldstein's *Wines of South America*. Catena had an immense influence on the improvement in quality in the Argentine wine industry and the subsequent Malbec boom that followed.

The Catena story starts with Nicola Catena who grew up in the Marches province of Italy and sailed to Argentina to seek prosperity. In 1902 he planted his first vineyard in Mendoza. Nicola's eldest son Domingo took over the business and continued to expand it.

It was under Nicolás that the company became a global force and helped redefine the Argentine wine industry. During a trip to California Catena became aware of the quality wines being made in California. Eager to replicate their success at home, he hired American wine consultant Paul Hobbs to work with his chief winemaker Jose' Galante and his viticulturist Pedro Marchevsky. He encouraged Hobbs to bring the winemaking and vine-growing practices into line with best practice California methods.

Catena made large investments in modern equipment such as temperature controlled stainless steel tanks that were needed to fight oxidation of the wine. He was also investing in research and development to an extent that was unheard of at the time. He experimented with high altitude vineyards by rigorous testing of different vine clones.

While originally focused on Cabernet and Chardonnay, Hobbs was able to convince him of the brilliance of Malbec. And once validated by high critical scores, Catena embraced Malbec as the grape of

Argentina.

Catena produces several ranges including the entry level Alamos range, Catena Zapata and the premium Nicolás Catena Zapata range.

We speak to winemaker Ernesto Bajda about the historic company.

Tell us about the history of Catena Zapata.

Nicolás Catena came to Argentina and established the Catena Winery in 1902. He was the first generation. Today we are on the fourth generation, led by Laura Catena. Nicolás' father Domingo Catena turned the wineries into a very big business. Then the third generation, Nicolás Catena brought high-quality standards to the wines. Laura Catena is maintaining that tradition, but also adding another component through research in winemaking and grape growing.

Many people view Nicolás Catena as a pioneer in Argentina in terms of promoting Malbec around the world.

Yes, I would say not only promoting Malbec, but making the world pay attention to Argentinian wines. He told the world that Argentina could produce outstanding wines that could be compared to any other wines. And with that, he introduced Malbec to the world. Malbec was not ever mentioned 30 years ago, and now it's one of the top five red grape players in the world. He also introduced different techniques and ideas that he brought from California, because he had spent some time in California. He changed dramatically the quality of the

wines, not only in the Catena Zapata family of wines, but also in the whole of Argentina. He introduced a small barrique. He introduced drip irrigation in the vineyards, stainless steel inside the wineries, so many different things that led him to have outstanding wines to say to the world, "Hello, this is Argentina. We can produce Malbec, and outstanding quality Malbec."

Nicolás Catena is described as a pioneer. What do you feel are his greatest achievements?

Well, first of all, he believed that Mendoza and Argentina had something special, and he started focusing on quality. Most of that is explained by the hierarchy condition that is unique. Everyone said that he was crazy when he planted Adrianna, our highest altitude vineyard, which is 5,000 feet above sea level. They all said he was going to lose and that he would not get a single grape from there because it was too high. When we saw the effect on the Malbecs that came from that area, we said there is something important about the altitude, and that's when we started to focus. He was the first person to make a Malbec plant selection from our vineyard in Angelica, a 90-year-old vineyard today. He found that there was something special about that vineyard, so he selected 145 plants, the best plants of the lot, and reproduced them in different areas. Enough that 20 years later, we are now working with five of those, after 20 years of starting them and choosing the top five of them. So things that were not made before, in terms of research and improving the quality.

And Laura Catena? She is the next generation. She's also an ER

doctor in San Francisco. How does she manage her life?

Well, if a day had 28 hours, she would probably use all of it. She works as an ER doctor and she's also very involved in the communication and conveyance of the wine in the US and worldwide. She also travels here several times a year when we taste the wines, make the blends, and release the vintages. So she's very active, very involved. She actually realized that her father needed help in communicating in the US market. So she said, "Okay, I'm going to help you," and that's how she slowly started getting more and more involved. And now she is the vice president of the company.

You grow grapes in multiple regions in Mendoza. Can you describe the different areas and how they're used?

The Catena Zapata family of wines sources grapes from what we consider the two best quality areas or valleys in Mendoza. One is what we call the prime region. In Spanish, *primera sona*. The area where everything started. It was the area closest to Mendoza, where they found the best quality. Then, over time and with new technologies, the growers are able to get water, and we were able to develop the Uco Valley and newer areas, younger areas. So now we are sitting in Agrelo, which is part of the "primera sona." We have, as I mentioned, in this prime region, the Angelica vineyard. The Angelica vineyard is a 90-year-old vineyard. The oldest vineyard of the family was named after Nicolás Catena's mother, Angelica. And it actually happens to be the mother of the rest of the vineyard because all the Malbec plants, all the materials that we planted in the rest of the vineyards, were taken from that vineyard. And we have four vineyards producing in Uco Valley, and two under development.

Everybody I talked to is talking about this one little area in Mendoza that is very exciting right now. Gualtallary. Is that something that you're working with right now?

Let me tell you this, Gualtallary was the first vineyard to be planted. Gualtallary was the Adrianna vineyard. It was our highest elevation vineyard planted by Nicolás Catena between 1993 and 1997. Everybody thought that Nicolás Catena was crazy planting it because they said he will never get a single berry from there because it was too cold and too high. And then it happened to be our best iconic vineyard. And probably one of the most studied vineyards in the world. Most of our research and knowledge on the high altitude effect was taken from that vineyard. We are running several research programs together with universities and research institutes, and they are all looking at Adrianna. And now we just planted a vineyard up the road, a bit higher. The Adrianna vineyard is 5,000 feet. The new

vineyard will be about 6,000, which is right at the limit.

The altitude, the fact that it's higher up gives a little bit more acidity and structure to the wine. Is that correct?

Absolutely. I call it high altitude, cool climate, desert. It's all combined. You have the high altitude that gives you lower temperatures during the day and very low temperatures during the night. You have sunlight because you are in a higher altitude, so you have less atmosphere to filter the sunlight. You have more sun effect. You have dry conditions because we have only eight inches of rain. Actually it varies, about 10 inches. Mendoza's average is eight inches, but it's a bit higher in some spots. But it is still very low.

We did an interview with Paul Hobbs recently, who was the first consulting winemaker at Catena. And he talked a little bit about how the Malbec boom started. He mentioned that originally it was Chardonnay that was going to be the grape that everybody thought would take Argentine wines to the

58

next level. He had worked on a small vineyard and created a Malbec. Then all of a sudden it got a big score, and that was the snowball going down the hill that started everything. Can you tell us a little bit about that time?

Yes, you are right. I would say that probably after Malbec, it would be different grapes, like Cabernet Sauvignon, or Chardonnay. We have something unique here, which is the higher altitude. That makes any grape variety, if you take good care, get fantastic results. I would say that Malbec was the start kick, how you say, the first kick, but there are many things coming on the back of that. Nicolás Catena's first two wines in the US market were the Catena Cabernet Sauvignon and the Catena Chardonnay. He knocked on many doors.

Actually, not only Nicolás, but his wife, Elena Catena. She went to different wine stores and said, "Okay, this is Cabernet Sauvignon and Chardonnay from Argentina." They said, "No, I am not interested." Then, "Okay, which is your best bottle of Chardonnay and which is your best bottle of Cabernet Sauvignon?" Catena said, "Well, this one and this one." They decided to taste them. They tasted them side by side. She was the first floor salesperson there and she got great results. That was about 1992, 1993. The first Catena Malbec released was the 1996 and yes, it was like that. It was a grape here in Mendoza, spread all around, called by the French, Malbec with a CK, others with just a K, but it was all around. There were plenty of old vineyards of that French variety. We normally use it as a back blender in the wines. Nicolás saw something special in that variety. There were different wineries doing small productions, but the big boom came when we could show the world what Malbec is like.

Ernesto, how much wine does Catena make right now? And how many different types of wine are you making at this moment?

The total production for Catena Zapata wines is about four million liters, counting both exports. That's about five million bottles all together, domestic and export markets. The domestic market is huge for us. It is based on the Catena label. Then we have the top of the line, which is a very limited, very small amount of each. The domestic market is now 60% of our production. In terms of variety, we focus on Malbec, which is about 55%, followed by Cabernet Sauvignon and in third place is Chardonnay. Those are the three main varieties. I would say that they are in total about 90 to 92%, and the rest is mostly for the domestic market and some labels for the rest of the world. We make Sauvignon Blanc. We make Cabernet Franc. Cabernet Franc is becoming very important for us. We are always doing something new. That's something that Laura is always encouraging. We are always thinking about something new to offer, to show.

What is the future? Do you have any interesting or exciting projects that you're working on?

Yes. Actually since I started here 11 years ago, we have never stopped developing and researching new ideas. The problem is, well it's not a problem, it's actually something good, is that it takes us about five or six vintages to release something before we're sure of it. The last releases were the two Chardonnay single vineyards coming from Adrianna vineyard, the White Stones and the White Bones. These are two whites focused on soil. We started working on them in 2006, but the first vintage release was 2009. Everything takes time, but we are constantly working on that. We are focused now on the Cabernet Sauvignon. Nicolás Catena is a big fan of the Bordeaux Cabernet Sauvignon. He really believes that Mendoza and the high altitude conditions that we have here in the soil in different parts of Mendoza, can provide an excellent opportunity for Cabernet Sauvignon. We are always working on some crazy things. Some sparkling, some Claret style wines, and other things that I can not mention because they're top secret. Because you can not leave here if you know....

Okay. Right. Well that's a little worrying. Are there things other than Malbec that you're super excited about right now?

I am personally excited about researching our local, traditional varieties like the Criolla, a high yielding variety. It was kind of like a Sangiovese. Sangiovese was very widely planted in Mendoza and Criolla was widely planted as well. But it was used more for bulk volume wine or for concentrates. We started studying good management in the vineyard. By using the right techniques in the winery, you can produce a very unique wine. We are also very linked by tradition to Mendoza's history.

That's awesome. If you were stuck on a desert island and you could only have one wine with you, one producer, and it wasn't Catena, what would it be?

I like Sherry. I'm a big fan also of GSM (a reference to red wines blended from Grenache, Syrah and Mourvèdre from the Rhône). Things like that.

J. Cobos s/n, Agrelo, Luján de Cuyo, Mendoza
+54 261 413 1100

http://www.catenawines.com

61

ANA BALBO
SUSANA BALBO WINES

Susana Balbo has played an important part in establishing Malbec as the international commercial hit. She is one of Argentina's great entrepreneurial stories. In 1981 she became the first woman in Argentina to receive a degree in enology. Before launching her own company, she worked in Cafayate, Salta province at the Michel Torino winery where she helped to put the Torrontés varietal on the map. Afterwards she worked at many well-regarded wineries including Catena Zapata and consulted internationally in Spain, Chile, Italy, Brazil, Australia and California.

After a first failed attempt to start the Lovaglio Balbo Winery in 1990 (which closed in 1994), she bounced back in 1999 when she launched Dominio del Plata which includes the brands Ben Marco and Crios as well as the Susana Balbo label. What is incredible about the business is that it is entirely export-focused, which in Argentina, a country with extremely high per capita wine consumption, is unusual. More than just creating good wine, Balbo has proved masterful at building brands. The company ethos is to spend four times on marketing what is spent on the core capital expenses of the winery.

Her children, José, a U.C. Davis-trained winemaker, and her daughter Ana decided to go on with the family tradition and join the Susana Balbo Wines team.

We talk to Ana Balbo about the family business and building an export-focused brand.

Ana, tell us about how your mother started this winery.

My mother started this winery in 1999. Actually, she began the business, the company in 1999 after the closure of her previous winery in 1994. She realized that she needed to build the business first, the actual winery - the building, the tanks, everything. In 1999, she began with two people and an office. She actually made wine in other wineries, renting a tank, and working for other people. Then she rented a little winery. After that, in 2001, she began building Dominio del Plata, the winery we own today, completing it in 2002.

My mother graduated from Don Bosco University here in Mendoza in 1991, and became the first female winemaker. It was quite difficult for her back then, because this was an industry, and still kind of is, dominated by men. Argentina is quite a traditional country; the division between women and men is still really traditional. Back then, she tried to find a job here in Mendoza as a winemaker but she couldn't. She was only offered a job as a lab assistant. She then made

63

her way to Salta in the extreme north of Argentina.

I don't know if they are less traditional there, or because it's quite the challenge to go and live in Cafayate, a small town in northern Argentina. She lived there for 10 years. When she moved there she was the lowest paid winemaker in the valley, and in a couple of years, she became the highest paid winemaker in the valley as a result of her hard work, her dedication, and the new ideas and techniques she brought to winemaking. That's how she began crafting Torrontés more than 30 years ago, and changed winemaking for us, and for Argentina. This is our flagship white variety.

Back then no one saw Torrontés' potential. A lot of producers just treated Torrontés as a table grape, and no one saw the international potential of its elegant style. My mother realized that through a careful process, she could take the bitterness through a turn test. Though it is quite aromatic it got really bitter in the mouth.

Then after spoiling many liters of Torrontés, she came up with the

64

idea of using some enzymes she learned about at university that were used for apple juice. She used them in Torrontés and she achieved a quite balanced and elegant wine. Her peers said, "Oh, Susana, what have you done? This is an elegant, feminine wine! This is not the Torrontés we're used to."

It's quite a thing to build a business and then fail at it and have the courage to get back on the horse and try again. How did she have the fortitude to try again?

I think it's a matter of character. She's really an entrepreneur and she is persistent - going forward, trying again, doing new things. I think the second time around, she realized she has learned a lot. Experience gave her the courage and the confidence to start again. Also, because she's quite independent and she needed to run her own business.

In terms of the failure of the first business and the success of the second business, what changed? What lessons did she learn that translated into making this business a success?

I think back then she learned that the first business was focused on the Argentina market. The Argentina market is really tricky. It's not as confident and it's difficult to get paid. It's difficult to trust people sometimes. Her second project, our winery at the moment, is 98% focused on export. The second thing she learned was that for every dollar she put in capitol, the building, the tanks, in everything, she needed four dollars to build her market. You cannot put all your savings, or all your money in, because it's really difficult to get credit here in Argentina. She didn't have a big investor behind her to help her. She had to be really efficient in how she spent her money.

She realized that she had to build a market first. She had to have demand for her wines first, and then build her company. That's how she did it. She began building the business, building demand, selling, promoting, traveling as much as she could. Then she was able to build the company. It's also a mixture between being a really capable entrepreneur and sometimes, you also have to have luck.

When my mother began in 2001 in Argentina, we had what was called a "Corralito." El Corralito was the informal name of an economic crisis in 2001, and the government froze all bank accounts. She was advised by someone with connections that the Corralito was about to happen. She had some savings from the sale of her previous company, her first winery. She had to sell for less than she anticipated. She told her bank manager to wire her money out, before that happened. When the Corralito occurred, she realized that her order was held up and that the money was still there, so she told the bank manager, "You have to do something because you promised, and I instructed you three months in advance to take my money out."

He said, "The only way I can give you your money is if you start spending." In 2001, Argentina was facing one of the worst crisis ever and she was building this winery because she had to spend money, so she started buying equipment, just to be able to access her money. She was poor back then. After 2001, Argentina had a big devaluation, and that was the big jump that enabled this company to grow, because the working capitol multiplied. The elevation happened like four times back then. That's how the business was able to grow - so sometimes you need a bit of luck too!

When you started, you were producing about 3,000 cases and now you're producing more than 200,000 cases. Is that correct?

Exactly.

How did that transition occur? That's pretty significant growth.

I don't know if it is luck, or perhaps the word is timing. When my mother started exporting from Argentina, there was not a favorite wine yet, but with her peers, other colleagues, other big wineries, they started building the category and she was part of the movement back then, 10 years ago when Argentina made a reputation for itself in the export market. I think she had great timing to start exporting. The demand for Argentina was growing rapidly, and obviously the quality of the wine was there to help to combine that growth. I think that's how it happened.

It's also a lot of hard work. Nothing happened from scratch. My mother travels. She still travels many days a year. We have 36 open markets, and every single one of them was opened by her - traveling, being present, working really hard.

In terms of the winery, how have things changed since you started? What sort of innovations have you embraced?

I think a lot of things have changed. We are a winery that is really open to change and really, really open to innovation. We have changed the way we work, we have gotten better, we have grown, we have built places to work more comfortably, we have invested in what we needed to make the best quality wines. Then what I consider is personally most important, is the team. My mother is a really great team builder. We have a great team here, a lot of young people, really professional and really committed to the winery. We know that good people are expensive, we don't mind. At the moment, we have

a really professional company even though we are a medium-sized, family business, this is a really professional company with really good professionals.

Our general manager, Edgardo del Popolo, is excellent. He's one of the finest viticulturists in Argentina. He has worked with big companies. He has a background in professional companies. Our winemakers, our CFO, we have built quite a structure despite being small, medium-sized, but we like things well done. I think that's one of our biggest changes. That also reflects my mother's spirit because she doesn't hesitate to hire someone that complements her skills. She's really good at some things, she is really an entrepreneur, but she's not an organized person. She's an entrepreneur. She's not afraid of hiring when things need to get done.

Ana, how has the winemaking changed over the years?

I think one of the most important advantages we have, is that we have really well-qualified people traveling around. We have my mother, a

winemaker, we have Eddie, a viticulturist and a winemaker, and my brother, who is also a winemaker and graduated from Davis. They're also in the market. We are able to make changes here really fast. When we see that trends are changing in the marketplace, and we see that consumers are asking for something different, this is a family business, there is no bureaucracy here, so they come back and say, "We have to do this, we have to change this."

I think winemaking has changed so far. We have a really consistent style of wines. We are really focused on quality and making wines that are enjoyed by consumers, that's our main aim. We don't want to get into extremes.

However, we are very focused on research, we travel a lot. For example, we travel to Australia to a highly technical conference that is held every three years. We travel to other wineries, to other regions to learn, and then on the other hand, we have been changing and investigating the sourcing of our grapes. At the moment, less harvest. The grapes are high-quality sourcing grapes and they are really high-quality grapes for wines and we put those grapes into Crios. Crios is a $15 retail wine. We don't mind doing that because we know that the best marketing is the quality in the bottle.

There seems to be a movement away from over-extracted, high alcohol Malbecs to wines that have more balance, a little bit more acidity, more structure.

Yes, that change has happened and is happening for sure. I think Argentina wants to move away from really high-concentrated wines, or really oaky wines, to wines that better express our terroir, and our sourcing, our land, and our country as a grape growing region. We are trying to produce wines that reflect the place we are coming from, and they express better, it's more about the fruit. It's more about what the soil can produce.

Fortunately, perhaps in a couple of years, because it will be a big job - in Argentina and Mendoza in particular - it's still not a well-defined area, like other regions. Some of them are already defined, but some of them aren't. At the moment, the law is not in place that would enable us to put the region on the front of the label, but we are moving forward. I think most of the wineries are aligned. Maybe in a couple of years? If there is a lot here in Argentina, in this region, we think, "Oh what's next, Malbec?"

Honestly, in my opinion, there are a lot of consumers that haven't even tried Malbec yet. I think there is a lot of work to be done there, but if we say what's next after Malbec, maybe Malbec! We cannot talk about Cabernet Franc as there are only 600 acres planted in Argentina through the sources of Malbec (more than 40,000 acres) that we have. What we can talk about is that Malbec from one terroir is not quite the same as Malbec from another terroir, and not quite the same as Malbec from Vista Flores. Maybe if you have three glasses of wine crafted from those regions, you can honestly notice the difference. I think we are working toward teaching and to showing consumers that we have real differences to reveal.

Cochabamba 7801Agrelo - Lujan de Cuyo, Mendoza
+54 261 498 9200

http://en.susanabalbowines.com.ar/

DAVID BONOMI
BODEGA NORTON

The Norton Winery has been on its existing site for more than a century. It was named for Edmund Norton, an English engineer who planted vines at the estate in 1895 and who was also the architect of the railway connecting Chile with Mendoza.

In 1989 Gernot Langes-Swarovski of Swarovski, the Austrian crystal dynasty, bought Bodega Norton. The business is run by his son Michael Hastrick.

We talk to Norton winemaker David Bonomi.

Tell us about Bodega Norton.

Bodega Norton is a winery in Mendoza in Argentina. It's a very important player in the wine industry. Now it's in the top five in our market and in the export market. Norton has always produced very high-quality wines.

When was the estate founded?

Bodega Norton was founded 120 years ago by James Palmer Norton. Now the Swarovski family owns the winery.

How many different winemakers do you think have been in charge of Bodega Norton over the years?

There are approximately five winemakers in charge of all the processes. No one winemaker is dedicated to or involved in all the processes. My boss is Jorge Riccitelli. He's the chief winemaker, and there are approximately four other winemakers who develop different activities in the winery.

You've been in business for over 100 years, how many different people do you think have been making wine at this

estate? There must have been many.

This is a very particular winery. There are a lot of employees that are family. Grandfathers, fathers and sons are related to this winery. This is a real family winery.

What is the winemaking philosophy at Norton?

The single most important factor is to maintain quality, quality, and quality year in and year out. In general, our most important wine is red. Our philosophy and the concept for Norton is to integrate all the aromas, the colors and amounts, to produce a very, very nice balanced wine.

Over the past 20 years, Malbec has exploded in the world arena. Argentina and Malbec are almost part of the same sentence now. Has that changed the mix of wines that have been made at Bodega Norton?

When Malbec began to explode, it was most important for us to well-integrate the vineyards with the winery or the winery inside the vineyards. For a long, long time, it was common practice for different producers to just put the grapes in the winery, and then the winemakers would produce the wine.

Now it's a mix. It's blending because it's most important to integrate the quality in the vines, in the winery, and the winery in the vines. This is the real challenge. When the Malbec explosion began, we started

71

to develop Malbec alone because for a long, long time, Malbec was blended in different red wines.

The owners are the famous Swarovski crystal family. How has their ownership changed the way that things operate in the winery? As an aside, I would imagine that you must get very good wine glasses in the tasting room.

For me, most importantly is that they love Argentina. They own land in southern Argentina. They first started visiting Patagonia, and then they began visiting other Argentine regions. When they arrived in Mendoza, they fell in love with this place, and with the wines. This is why they founded or re-founded Norton, approximately 25 years ago, and then introduced the philosophy of very high-quality wines.

You mentioned you make 60 different wines. That's a lot of wine to keep track of over a year. How do you focus on all of those wines, and ensure that quality is paramount?

I think that it's very important that you visit our winery. There are different steps. There are different tanks, barrels and different facets of management in the winemaking process. The most important is when I work with our Norton collection, it's for wine you can drink every day. It's important for us to put the "chips" inside the wine and work with this wine. When this activity is completed, I'll take out these "chips" and put the "chip" aside for this particular activity. It is critical to be focused on all the details of the work.

You mentioned earlier that the ownership is very supportive of experimentation and trying new things. Having 60 wines indicates that you are open to trying new things. Talk about the spirit of experimentation.

It is a wonderful experience for us because our owners are very open-minded. I can start working on a small idea and I can develop it very easily because they support it economically, or they support all the people that help me, or help our team in developing this idea. It's very easy because the owners maintain a very healthy company and then continue to run it.

Talking a bit more about exploration and innovation, what are some of the new things that you can point to that you are excited about developing?

First, when I think about new ideas, I always think about place - terroir. I'd have to check this place, and then start to be very open-minded in the winemaking process for this specific terroir because it's a completely different winemaking process for the other range of drinks

- very easy for the thirst-quenchers, and it's completely different than when I go to south of the range or aging in barrels, or look for a specific terroir.

Are there any varietals other than Malbec that you're very excited about? Everybody talks about Malbec, but you make 60 different wines.

For us it is Perdriel, you are in Perdriel now; Norton is the heart of Perdriel. The most important beside that is Cabernet Sauvignon. This place is very, very spectacular for growing Cabernet Sauvignon. But now we are starting to work in a very small area with Cabernet Franc. We have only planted a very small amount but it's a very nice varietal to develop. In white, Chardonnay is good and the second most planted varietal for white is Sauvignon Blanc. We also have continuous development of Viognier, Reisling, and Semillon, for example.

When I start to speak of these white varietals in general we go to the Uco Valley. Norton started working in the Uco Valley approximately three or four years ago with different farmers because in the future, we will start to buy small parcels of land or small vineyards in Uco for our property development, but now I buy different grapes from different producers from Uco. Uco is a very high altitude area. The average altitude is 3,300 feet and for white varieties, it's very nice.

Ruta 15 - km 23,5
Perdriel, Luján de Cuyo
Mendoza
+54 261 490-9700

http://www.norton.com.ar

GUSTAVO ARIZU
LUIGI BOSCA

The Arizu family can trace their ancestry back to the 18th century to a small village in the Basque country. Leoncio Arizu arrived in Argentina in 1890 and founded the winery in 1901 with an old Piamonte family called the Boscas. The winery is now in the hands of his grandchildren and great-grandchildren. The estate is located in the Luján de Cuyo region of Mendoza, however the firm owns seven vineyard sites in diverse areas including the Uco Valley, Luján de Cuyo and Maipú.

Bodega Luigi Bosca has begun to work with the philosophy of biodynamics and biodiversity by adding other plants such as olive and chestnut trees.

We speak to fourth generation Gustavo Arizu about the evolution of the family.

Gustavo, tell us about the history of your family.

This winery was launched in 1901. We are the fourth generation of the family. Leoncio Arizu was the first generation who came to Argentina from Spain in 1893. He settled in San Rafael.

He then moved to Luján de Cuyo to find better soil conditions, to produce excellent wines, high-quality wines. The third generation is running the company today. The fourth generation, my generation, is managing the expansion of the winery.

Tell us about the terroir here at Luján de Cuyo.

When my great-grandfather decided to move to Argentina, he did so on the strength of the Argentine economy at the time. Then, Argentina was one of the fastest growing countries in the world. The idea was

74

to come to a place where there were similar conditions to where the family came from. He arrived in San Rafael because many of the train lines went to San Rafael and because he had family there. But he moved to Luján de Cuyo when he discovered the conditions of the terroir there. The altitude in Luján de Cuyo starts at 850 meters and rises to 1200, giving it excellent soil conditions. The soil and the water conditions are ideal for producing high-quality wines.

The terroir in Luján de Cuyo is made of limestone, with also a small amount of clay. That drives the roots deep into the soil. At about a meter to a meter and 20, depending on the area, one finds a layer of chalk and clay, which creates a low pH in the soil. Lower than eight causes the wine to have a lower pH during the process of maturation. It helps to produce healthy wines. Also, it produces a wine that can age for longer periods of time.

You're the fourth generation. There aren't that many fourth generation wine families in Argentina these days. What's it like being part of that heritage? Was there ever a time when you thought, "I want to be a race car driver, screw the wine business?" Or has it always been something you knew from a

75

very young age that you were excited to be a part of?

Perhaps it's because of our history and identifying with and appreciating the different generations. The business was always in family hands and part of our history is a belief in producing high-quality wines. That's why so many members of our family have joined the business. As the fourth generation, we're still in the family business. There were many periods in which the wine industry suffered in Argentina. Also, we reached consumption of 90 liters per capita. Now it has dropped to 30 liters per capita. Yet the consumer demands high quality.

Today, what is most important to our family heritage is producing wines in Mendoza. We are dedicated to maintaining our brand here in Mendoza. We are a family company; it is part of our life. Over 70% of our time is devoted to the company. It's the wine. It's the brand, and protecting it. It's very important for us because we are proud to belong to a company that settled in Argentina. We are proud to produce Argentine wines.

Gustavo, can you describe how things have changed in Mendoza over four generations? For example, Malbec has all of a sudden exploded all over the world. Everybody knows Argentine Malbec, whereas 20 years ago it wasn't really known. How has that changed the way people produce wines in Mendoza?

Many years ago Argentines consumed 90 liters per capita, now it has dropped to 30. But, the consumers still want high-quality wines. And, wines that age for longer periods. In the beginning, the consumption of Malbec Cabernet Sauvignon was higher, in comparison to Malbec. But today, the consumer wants a more elegant type of wine. Cabernet Sauvignon is a great wine, but Malbec is a more plastic wine. It's where you can show your potential, as a family and as winemakers. You can show it in Malbec. That's why consumption of Malbec increases, because of people visiting Argentina. Also, the consumer in Argentina today wants this mature, soft, juicy, attractive type of wine. Malbec fits that description.

You told me a little earlier that your family has gone from making one million bottles of wine to seven million bottles of wine in your generation. How has that impacted the way the family does business? Has it changed the way that you make wine?

First, it's important to note that this growth has evolved over time. In the beginning of the one-million-and-a-half, 90% was for the domestic market, and 10% was exported.

When Argentina began exporting high-quality wines, there were many importers interested in Argentine wines. The first generation was that generation that normally is disruptive. It's the generation that said, "Okay, this is not the only market that we have. We have many countries around the world that we can introduce our wines to."

The first generation was the one that exported wines from the company I started 20 years ago, and my brother started 26 years ago. When he started, he was introducing wines to markets like Finland and Brazil. They were the first markets to where we exported wine. They were completely astonished with the quality of our wines.

Everybody knows Malbec. Argentina and Mendoza are almost synonymous with the Malbec grape. What other varietals do you think really illustrate the terroir of Mendoza?

Well, Mendoza has a potential for many different varieties. One of the varieties that now has the same potential is Cabernet Franc. The plasticity of Cabernet Franc makes it ideal for winemakers and wineries. It's a variety that can manage many different styles. Dry, soft. Dry flowers. Brown color or red color, fruity. We can have a very fruity type of Cabernet Franc. Cabernet Franc has the plasticity. We will just

Cabernet Sauvignon can produce great wines. Cabernet Franc has the plasticity. We will just see how it can be updated or how it can play with different varieties.

Just to jump back to the previous question, you've grown from a million to seven million bottles. Is there ever a concern that the quality will slip as you get bigger? Is that something that you worry about?

No. The jump that we made from that million to seven million was done in a way that allowed us to maintain quality. If we look at the figures, they reflect the jump because of the consumption in imports. Perhaps, we jumped at that time from one to 20, but we jumped in a way in which we also managed quality. We are always focused on quality, because the most important thing is to support the consumer as well as the brand. If we lost quality by increasing production, sooner or later we would jump from one to 10 and then to three. The idea was to jump every step that we made making sure it was solid. As solid as the way that we manage production in the vineyards. Solid in the quality. Solid in the markets, and in our relations with our importers.

San Martin 2044 , Lujan de Cuyo , Mendoza
+54 261 498-1974

http://luigibosca.com.ar

MENDOZA, ARGENTINA

MAX TOSO
HUARPE

Huarpe is owned by brothers Max and José Toso. They are part of the Toso wine family which owns Luigi Bosca. Max runs the business as general manager and Jose' is the winemaker.

José had previously worked as a winemaker in Europe for six years. He was chief winemaker at J. Hofstaetter Winery in Alto Adige, Italy and winemaker at the Graf Adelmann Winery in Baden-Württemberg, Germany. Max has a business background and previously worked as a consultant at McKinsey & Co. in Argentina.

The Huarpe winery is located in Agrelo, Mendoza's first viticultural area. It is at the foothills of the Andes, and has alluvial soils, and its climate consists of cool nights and warm days.

Max, tell us about Huarpe. How did you and your brother start this winery?

We were literally born in a winery. Our family has been in the wine business for a very, very long time, but Huarpe is a new project. José was returning after a decade in Europe and I was trying to quit consulting, and so we decided to start Huarpe in 2003, putting together our backgrounds as wine people. We know Mendoza and now we're trying to help in the development of Argentine wines in international markets.

What's the philosophy of winemaking at Huarpe?

The key is to pay attention to our terroirs, in combination with our district and what we are trying to capture up front. Agrelo is our home,

80

but we are also making wines in the Maipú area and the Uco Valley. We are trying to express our terroir by using the best technology available.

Tell us about Agrelo. Why did you choose Agrelo to be the home base for the winery?

Agrelo is a high altitude area, so you cannot have a high yield here, yield is controlled by altitude in this district, which is also is known as the capital of Malbec. Malbec is home here in Agrelo. We're not that creative. There are a lot of big brands around us, so it was kind of an easy choice.

Tell us a little bit about the terroir of Agrelo.

Agrelo has an alluvial soil system, very deep alluvial soil with a balance of clay, sand, and silt. You have to go down about 10 feet to hit ground rocks, so there is a lot space to develop a root system. It is also a very cold area, not only because of the altitude, but also because of the flow of air. It's going down from the Andes mountains which we have on the west and we have a small hill on the east, so the air gets stuck and this make it very cold, and we really like cold weather wines.

You do some very interesting blends. Tell us about the

philosophy behind the blends.

The three top districts that we work in are Agrelo, Maipú and Uco. We asked ourselves what the best blend is that we could produce in this area. So in Agrelo, the answer was easy. It should be a blend based on Malbec, and the best grape blend for Malbec is Cabernet Sauvignon. We're trying to add Malbec as the backbone and Cabernet Sauvignon for its spicy notes. In the case of Maipú, we think of Maipú as one of the best Cab areas, and Merlot as the best grape blend for Cabernet Sauvignon.

We think the Uco Valley is the best area for grapes that require a long maturation period, such as Bonarda and Petit Verdot. Bonarda and Petit Verdot are a great pair because you have both the fruit character of Bonarda and then the floral notes of Petit Verdot together with the tannin content, and you also have balance and structure with these two grapes.

Your brother was a winemaker in Germany and in Italy. How has his European experience influenced winemaking in Mendoza and helped you make a truly Argentine wine?

I think you have several influences in Argentina, and this is what is to be Argentinian. It's a country of immigrants, as yourself, you are Argentinian, right?

That's correct.

An immigrant! So we have a lot of different influences. Obviously, the European influence is very strong, and so we were searching for wines with balance, not highly extracted wines, but wines with elegance and balance. I think that is very European.

Max, tell us what you think are the most exciting things going on in the Argentine wine industry right now.

I think what we are doing right now is showing the world that we are much more than Malbec, and that Argentine winemaking is very diverse. Maybe we are not viewed that way in the world, so we need to communicate it. Now we are showing our diversity. We are also producing great Cabernet Sauvignon, Bonarda, white grapes, sparkling, so this is the most interesting part. Showing the world what we can produce. Diversity is the key.

You make a Pinot Noir which is interesting. Tell us about the Pinot Noir that you make.

Basically when José returned from Europe, he was talking about Pinot Noir, and everyone here was talking about Malbec. He thought

in Argentina our wine industry is so huge that there is a place for everything, for every grape. We just need to find it. So we did a lot of trials, in different areas, and after a lot of mistakes, we found a vineyard in Vista Flores which is great for Pinot Noir, and we are producing a more European style. Traditionally, the Argentinian Pinot Noir was heavier and darker in color. We are trying to do a real Pinot Noir, with more character.

What's next for Huarpe?

Right now, we have the new Huarpe terroirs and this is where our growth is going to come from in terms of products. We have 17 different wines, which is a lot for a winery of our size, but blends and terroir for different blends is our focus in terms of product. We serve 11 different markets, but we are always trying to expand to new areas in the world. Always small volume channels, we are not serving big accounts. We service independent liquor stores, restaurants, and we even do direct sales in different part of the world. In terms of markets, our focus is to try to take Huarpe to many more different places and geographies.

How have you grown since you started? You're doing 40,000 cases now, that's not a huge winery but it's a good, medium-sized winery.

Grape Collective's Christopher Barnes talking with Max and José Toso

Exactly. Our growth rate has been very fast. But José has a lot of experience in growing output each year. In his previous job, he actually moved a winery from about less than a million bottles per year to five million bottles per year, and he even got a prize for increasing quality. We are not going that far, but we have experience, and most importantly we have a great supply.

Right now we produce more grapes than we are using, and so we still can grow, let's say about twice our size, but not more than that, because we will keep our idea that we need a guy to explain the wines. Our story cannot be told with only our bottle, you need a wine geek in front communicating, and you only get these people in the small volume channels. So we need to partner with these people and this is something we will not change with growth.

You're building a complex here, how would you describe it?

That's another challenge. In Argentina, financing is always a challenge and when a wine business grows, you need to invest a lot of capital. Obviously, you will never pay a dividend in the early stages of the project. We were very successful in entering a few markets, so now we need to invest a lot in the winery. You cannot get long-term financing here, so it always has to come from one's internal cash flow. Now, we are investing in client reception infrastructure. We need space for events both small and large, lodging facilities, and we would like to have a chef so we can create an experience for tourists.

Ruta Provincial 15 - Km 32
(5509) Agrelo, Luján de Cuyo
Mendoza
+54 261 4790222

http://www.huarpewines.com

FACUNDO PEREIRA
CASA BIANCHI

Don Valentin Bianchi, the founder of Casa Bianchi Winery, was born in 1887 in Fasano, Italy. He moved to Argentina in 1910 setting up his own winery in 1928 called "El Chiche Winery." The vineyards and winery are located in the San Rafael District, 150 miles south of Mendoza City, in the province of Mendoza. The company is now run by the fourth generation of the family, and has expanded to an operation with 865 acres of vineyards, 15 different varieties and exports to 40 countries.

We talk to winemaker Facundo Pereira about Malbec and the incredible growth of Casa Bianchi.

Tell us about Casa Bianchi and the history of this estate.

Casa Bianchi is a very traditional winery. It was started by Valentin Bianchi, who founded the winery. He arrived from Italy in 1910 because his brother lived in San Rafael. He recognized that Argentina was a land of opportunity. He initially worked at different jobs and in different situations until 1928. Then he achieved a dream he had for many years, to build a winery. He started a winery with his brother-in-law. For many years, he produced wine with a very nice philosophy - to be the smallest winery of the big wineries.

With this objective and this philosophy, he developed many wines according to the styles of the wines that the different wineries were producing at that time. An opportunity arose during the '40s to participate in an official contest of wines in the city of Mendoza. He produced some samples, and he won first prize in this tasting. Everybody at that time knew the winery, and they were coming to San Rafael to see that there was really a winery here. At that time, the

winery was called El Chiche because it was the name of a horse that Valentin Bianchi favored.

After that, people believed that the winery was real, that it existed. He got a very good prize and a very high score with the wines that he produced. After that, Valentin Bianchi and Bodega Chiche began producing and exporting wines. It was one of the first wineries to export wine to Europe because the family had ties with Italy; the owner came from Italy.

The winery continued to develop in the hands of the next generation. The founder's son, Enzo Bianchi took over the winemaking. After developing many products, he started to develop a wine that we call Don Valentin Lacrado. This is the main product that we produce. It is an eclectic Argentine wine. It is a wine that is 56 years old with a very high success rate. After creating this wine, Enzo Bianchi gave his son, Valentin Bianchi Jr., the opportunity to produce Altagama wines for Valentin Bianchi; to produce Enzo Bianchi which is an homage to Enzo, his brother, and his father. After this, they started to produce more Altagama wines and further develop the market. We are presently in more than 30 countries in the world.

What is your background as a winemaker.

I am currently in charge of all the winemaking at Casa Bianchi, since 2011. Before working here at Casa Bianchi, I spent a long time and gained very good experience in the Uco Valley with the group Clos De Los Siete.

That's Michel Rolland's company?

Yes, Michel Rolland's winery. In 2002 we had the first harvest, but it

began in 1997. We developed the character of Argentine wines, but with the French style of making wine. We mixed mainly the Malbec with the knowledge of the French method of making wine.

When you moved to Valentin Bianchi, did you take some of those French influences with you?

Yes, actually it is one of the reasons why I am here in Casa Bianchi. The founder and his sons Enzo and Valentin like the style very much.

Enzo and his brother Valentin always follow the philosophy of the founder. They always had a very good impression of French wines, in general. The style and philosophy is to produce wines with a very good character of each variety. Good balance and elegance is the first objective in producing wines. We embrace the French style of producing wine.

What is the philosophy of wine making of Valentin Bianchi?

Our philosophy is based on our founder's, and what he strove to give each of the different generations. This is to produce wines that respect the quality of independence of the level of wine of the concentration of expression and character that you want. Always produce wine with good, good quality. Accordingly, create a very good relation between the price and the quality that we offer in our different lines.

We start with very simple wines, very drinkable wines that you can drink every day, that we call our classic wines. And then we arrive at very complicated wine like Enzo. It is very elegant with very different details and character each time that you put your nose to the glass. You can taste the different notes, and it is always a different situation that expresses in the wine. If we look at both kinds of wine, we always accentuate quality. We are getting very good feedback from our customers. This is the basis of our philosophy.

Accordingly, we want each wine to have balance and elegance, this is what we respect. Each level of wine is different from the other according to the concentration and the complexity of the expression. In each line, you will find an elegant and balanced wine.

How has the winemaking changed over the last few years?

Over the last few years, we changed the concept of how to manage the states, and how we manage the oak in the wine because in the past, we had a very good and high presence of oak in the wines. Last year, we migrated to it becoming more of a complement to the fruit and the character of wine, to be closer to the concept of elegance and balance. This is the basis. After this, it was a question of managing and recognizing the different expressions in different states and to separate the different parts of the process in order to obtain the best result of each expression.

What do you think of the concept of modern winemaking in Mendoza?

That is a very good question! Actually, what we want is balance. The balance is not one side or the other. It's not the over-redness, it's not the green harvest. That is to say, we must be more consistent. I think that during the last 20 years we started to produce very heavy wines, very dark wines.

Actually, I think this is part of the philosophy of being elegant or being balanced. I think that in excess you become tired. The customer gets tired if we continue to always produce heavy wines. With this wine, when we go to the redness and the over-redness, it results in high alcohol. To not be an alcoholic wine, you must be a very hard wine.

Consequently, to know that is to try a different method. The idea is to pick early, but not too early. They start to feel green and tangy, so green expression. I think that balance is trying to find a good compromise between the good expression of fruit and the good expression in the mouth. This is, in my opinion, to arrive at a very good expression of wine.

Comandante Torres 500 - M5600BCJ
San Rafael, Mendoza
+ 54 0260 444 8500

http://www.casabianchi.com.ar/

AURELIO MONTES JR.
KAIKEN

Kaiken is owned by Montes, the Chilean winery headed up by iconic winemaker Aurelio Montes. They named their Chilean venture Kaiken, after the wild geese that are indigenous to Patagonia and fly over the Andes between Chile and Argentina. The firm is run by Aurelio Montes Jr., who moved full time to Chile in 2011 to oversee the Kaiken project.

We talk to Aurelio Montes Jr. about his influences as a winemaker and what it is like being a Chilean making wine in Mendoza.

Aurelio, you come from a very famous winemaking family. What was it like to grow up with a father who is considered the most important winemaker in Chile?

It's a big advantage to grow up with a father who has a lot of passion in his life. It is the best school! You can study winemaking anywhere, but passion can't be taught. My father is the best example of living a passionate life with wine.

Do you feel any pressure because of your father's reputation?

At the beginning, yes. At the beginning people said, "Oh he's the son of Aurelio Montes," but to be honest with you, people understood very quickly that I am a different person, I have my own style and my own personality. In the beginning, yes, but I never felt that people looked at me differently as a winemaker.

When you were growing up did you feel that there was an expectation that you would join the family business? You're one of five children, right?

Exactly. My father always dreamed, as I do with my kids, that someone in the family would join the business. Winemaking is not only a business, it is a passion. Everyone dreamed that one day one of us would follow in our father's footsteps and preserve the tradition. Of course, my father tried, in a very simple, strategic way to involve me in the wine industry. My other siblings do not really have the passion. They love to drink wine, but they understand that to be a winemaker you need to be passionate and devote your life to it; it's a lifestyle. I am the only one of my siblings that has that passion. Even today, I'm very passionate about what I do. I'm training my kids for the future, hopefully!

How did you evolve into the role of winemaker?

I am a country boy. I have always been interested in the outdoors. I love to ride horses, motorcycles and all things outdoors. My father positioned me in this business, step by step. I decided to study agriculture and engineering at university. In my last two years I studied winemaking purely out of curiosity. I wanted to understand why my father was so passionate about wine. I thought, there must be something to it. And, at least I needed to understand.

To be honest with you, at that time at university, I drank very little wine, almost none. I was more focused on sports and perhaps beer.

But when I studied winemaking and understood the processes and the world view of wine, I really started to fall in love with it. I moved to Australia and lived there for a year. I definitely found my passion there. Then I worked in Napa where I had a lot of fun. Perhaps not a great deal of experience in the wine industry, but I had a lot of fun meeting people going to parties, but also learning about wine. For me, that was the beginning.

Who were some of the mentors, other than your father, that kind of helped spark your flame that got you where you are?

There are a few winemakers who were really an important part of my education, of my experience. Phillip Shaw from Rosemount and then John Duval, also from Penfolds, who now has his own wine and consulting business for many wineries. These two winemakers, besides of course my father, have been mentors in terms of philosophy of work, or being efficient, and being passionate about what you do. Learning to take care of all the small details. That is what I learned from the three winemakers.

You started Kaiken in 2002. What was the idea behind that?

Kaiken was born, as you said, in the year 2002. Many people think that we moved to Argentina because it's very close to Chile; that's incorrect. We're winemakers. We don't care to fly. We don't care to go to places. After my father and I visited Australia, New Zealand, Italy, France, Spain, Napa, we realized that Argentina was the most extreme and new country at the time. We decided to go to a really new area, one that was really underdeveloped. We all have to develop it, and to learn. When we moved there, we found a country with passion, with a unique terroir, high altitude plantations, beautiful Malbecs and other varieties, so it was a perfect place to stay. Since that time, we have been growing. In the year 2011, I moved to Mendoza, Argentina, so I am living with my family, with my kids and my wife.

Argentina has a very strange political climate regarding the wine industry. You can't ship wine into Argentina, is that correct?

The importations of any product is almost forbidden. The political atmosphere and economy in Argentina is not helping the wine industry. Today investments are almost zero in the industry; not only us, but everyone stopped investing money in the wine industry. Why? Because today, with 40% inflation, you can't get any currency other than pesos. You can't buy dollars; you can't buy euros.

The economy's getting really complicated. We're not competitive.

We're trying the best we can to be as competitive as possible. Each year is getting more and more complicated. If the administration doesn't change, it's going to be tough for the wine industry.

You are very focused on the external market. You distribute something like 96% outside of Argentina. That's very unusual, isn't it, for an Argentine winery?

It is. It's very unusual. As Montes, we have the expertise to sell wine externally. As a company, as Kaiken, we sell to around 65 countries around the world, including Dubai, Hong Kong, Japan, the United States, almost everywhere in Latin America, Cook Islands, Maldives ... 65 countries. That's very strange in Argentina. The average winery in Argentina sells to five countries, but we sell in 65 countries. We're very unique in that regard. I am very proud to show Argentine wines to the world. Why keep them only in Argentina? There are a lot of people that want to drink Argentine wines. We feel very proud of being able to do that.

Let's talk about Malbec and Argentine wines. When you first came to Argentina, what were you trying to accomplish by building the winery? What sort of wines were you trying to make and how did you go about finding the areas to source your grapes?

To be honest, when we moved to Argentina, we didn't know much about Argentina. That was the most exciting part because everything was new to us. We decided not to buy even one acre of vineyards. We decided to buy grapes for the first eight years. When we went to Argentina, we tried different varietals. Of course, like many other people, we fell in love with Malbec. Unique in terms of its beautiful color. We also really love Cabernet Sauvignon and fell in love with Cabernet Franc, Sauvignon Blanc, Petit Verdot, Bonarda.

There are other varietals besides Malbec that work perfectly in Mendoza. The big difference between Malbec and the rest of the varietals in Mendoza is that Malbec is good almost everywhere. For other varietals, you need to find the right place. I always joke that Malbec is only for lazy winemakers because it's so easy to find a good place. Cabernet Sauvignon, Cabernet Franc, and other varietals, you need to work. You need to shovel, to analyze the soil, to find the right place, and we're a new country, so we don't have 1,000 years' experience. We're still in the learning stages and every year we find new things, new styles, new places to plant. Water is getting complicated now, but Argentina is still boiling in terms of new things coming up.

In terms of the wine culture, people have been talking about a modern approach to wine. A leaner, lower alcohol style, with a little bit more finesse, which in European countries would be described as a more traditional approach to wine. What do you think of the modern versus traditional winemaking dichotomy in Argentina?

That's a very good question. In Argentina, as I told you, we are still learning. We're still in the process of learning, so now you're going to find different type of wines. It's funny because, as you said, the new styles that European people showed us, okay, the New World countries are producing the new style of wines, and now in Argentina it is a normal style, and the new style is going back to the old style. It's a little confusing, but we're going back to our roots. We're going back more to the fruit: less oak, less alcohol, more fruit, more spiciness, more personality in the wines. Today, it's confusing, but inside Argentina we call the new style, the old style.

What is your personal philosophy of winemaking?

My philosophy, first of all, is to express the real taste of the terroir, of the place where I live. For me, terroir is not only climate and soil. Every place has a terroir, wherever you go, Venezuela, Colombia, wherever you go, has a terroir. A good terroir is a good expression of a unique place for wine. That is what I love to find, the one I love to express.

Not only that, but for me my style is to produce good wines. I love to drink wine. I'm first a consumer and then a winemaker. I love to drink wine, so I am looking for new things. It could be a little crazy or more traditional but I'm looking for a wine that is friendly, with soft tannins and beautiful acidity; wine that really has personality. I hate producing wines that taste common. I love a wine that has personality, when you drink it, you say, "Wow. I want another glass." That's the kind of wine I love. My philosophy is adding passion to the wine, not only making liquid with alcohol, making wine with personality and adding not only soil and water but adding also humans. We make a huge difference in the process. If someone from France goes to Argentina, of course the result's going to be different because he was born in another country, and with a different type of food. In Argentina, we love to show off what we have within our own culture.

Talking about people from different countries coming to Mendoza, there have been many. You have Paul Hobbs here; you have French estates. There seems to be a convergence on Mendoza, when it was heating up and everybody was buying Malbec. You're from Chile, which is a neighbor and sometime rival of Argentina. What was your experience coming from Chile and planting your stake in the ground in Argentina?

It's funny. We're neighbors, that's true. We always compete because we're neighbors. We need to compete. To be honest with you, for us, the wine industry is completely different from politics. When I go to Italy, or France, whenever I go and I tell the winery that I'm a winemaker, the doors open wide to receive us. The same is true in Argentina. In Argentina, the wine industry is very friendly. They are very warm and charming people.

At first, when I moved to Argentina, I was a little bit afraid. I thought, "What's going on here, are they going to receive us? Are they going to be rude to us?" But from the first day they said, "Come here, join us." They really like us, they love us, because we're a great supporter, a great promoter, and we do a lot of marketing for Argentina, for our wines, because we export everywhere. We're adding more now, in our new labels, we are including the Argentina flag. They love that, being Chilean, we're promoting Argentine wines with so much energy. They are very friendly to us, very friendly.

In terms of the future of Argentina, everybody seems to be talking about the Uco Valley and the fact that there are high altitude vines that are producing wines with more finesse. Specifically, Gualtallary is a name that I keep hearing. Is it a trend or is where the best wines are being made right now?

If you want to understand Argentina, especially Mendoza, you have to understand that we're new. Every time something new is discovered, it's like when you hear that there's a new restaurant that's just opened; everyone wants to go there. The chef is a new chef, someone told me that the food is very good. I'm not saying that Uco is bad. Quite the opposite, it's very good, but it's one style. If you ask me, "Aurelio, if I have to invest, is this place I need to go?" No. Not necessarily. It depends on how you like the wines.

Uco has one style that is very elegant with beautiful acidity, but that doesn't mean that the rest of Mendoza is horrible. It's a different style. There are plenty of top wines that don't come from Uco and the top ratings in the top magazines around the world are not all from Uco. They are from different places. In the end, depending on the variety, and Uco is huge, it's like Napa. There are some places in Napa that are not good, and some places in Napa that are amazing. Uco's the same. If you ask me, Uco, is it the place to be, not necessarily. I like it there, I love it, I love it there, but only as part of one of my styles. If I made all my wines there, I know it would be a hobby. I prefer to be more diverse.

What are the things that made Kaiken successful?

I think two things. The first thing is that we really try to produce wines with a lot of personality and we try to reflect the terroir, the real taste of Argentina. I always say, "But, Argentina maybe doesn't taste like the rest of the world." We're not aliens. We love to eat meat, we love barbecues, we have some special tastes that we love and I think that is very universal. I try to express that real terroir from Argentina.

Second, we always try to be very consistent in our wine. We're very responsible when we make a wine. For us, it's not a game. It's a profession. It's a wine passion. It's a lifestyle. When we make a wine from one year to another, for sure there will be some differences because of the year, but the line, the quality, the concentration, the elegance of the wine is going to be mainly the same. For me, those are the two more important keys for us. Representing the country from the very depth, and being consistent.

Other than Malbec, are there other varieties that you're excited about?

Definitely, yes. For example, shortly I am going to launch a new Cabernet Franc, 100% Cabernet Franc. I'm really, really crazy about it. We just launched a new Sauvignon Blanc. For me, a variety that is going to make a lot of noise in the future is Petit Verdot. Cabernet Sauvignon for me is really good, but in a completely different style from Bordeaux, Napa or Chile. It's different. Soft tannins, easy drinking, but the biggest problem for Argentina is that most of the Cabernet that is planted is planted in the incorrect places. Most of the Cabernet that we find in the market in Argentina is not so good, but when you find good ones, like Vistalba, it's like ice cream, like cream; very nice. Really, really nice. I think there are many things, like Torrontés from the north, coming in Argentina. Not all the varietals are going to work perfectly. For example, for me, Pinot Noir. I'm not excited about Pinot Noir in Argentina. Merlot in some places. Not everything works perfectly in Argentina, but Cabernet Franc, Malbec, Cabernet Sauvignon, Petit Verdot are perfect.

Where do you see the future of wine in Argentina?

The future of the wine industry in Argentina is very hard to define because we're very connected with the political decisions. I think we have plenty to present, plenty to grow. For example, Argentina is unknown in Asia. Argentina is barely even known in Europe. We still have plenty of markets to develop. Plenty of places to find new terroir wines, but the government doesn't allow us to invest. Things get really complicated. I'm not saying that they need to help us; but don't bother us. Let us grow, let us develop. If they did, Argentina would grow much more because people need to know that Argentina is more than Malbec.

Roque Saenz Peña 5516
(access through Callejón de la Virgen),
Vistalba, Mendoza,

+54 261-4761111

http://www.kaikenwines.com

MENDOZA, ARGENTINA

UP & COMING WINEMAKERS

By Amanda Barnes

While Malbec still reigns supreme in Argentina, there are a host of new up-and-coming producers who are putting a different foot forward in the market and showing that there are many more varieties to discover from this Latin American country. Here Amanda Barnes takes a look at some new (and re-invented!) producers to discover from Argentina.

Plop

Some of the most innovative winemakers in Argentina are the Michelini brothers (Matias and Juan Pablo) who are responsible for brands including Passionate Wines, Super Uco and Zorzal, and have led the way in making fresher, acidity-driven wines from the Uco Valley. Now it is the turn of their talented nephew Manuel to raise a few eyebrows in the wine world. Manuel may only be 19 but winemaking clearly runs in his blood (his mother Andrea Mufatto and father Gerardo Michelini are the celebrated winemakers of Ji Ji Ji/Gen) as the oenology student has released two of his own wines under the label 'Plop'. A light and refreshing rose from Cabernet Franc, and a racy red Malbec and Cabernet Franc blend with fresh fruit and a crunchy acidity. All eyes will be on the youngest Michelini to see where the future of winemaking leads him.

Twitter: @Manuelmichelini

Cara Sur: Francisco Bugallo, Nuria Añó Gargiulo, Marcela Manini, Sebastián Zuccardi

Cara Sur

There's something special brewing up in the high hillsides of Barreal.
A lesser-known micro wine region in the San Juan province up among
the beautiful Andes mountains, Barreal is filled with old Pergola vines
of somewhat-overlooked varieties like Muscat, Criolla and Argentine
Bonarda. Avid climber and winemaker Pancho Bugallo started making
wine up there with his brother as a hobby, but when his brother
Santiago moved to work in Salta, they enlisted the help of a friend,
who happens to be one of Argentina's top young-gun winemakers:
Sebastián Zuccardi. Together with their wives, Pancho and Sebastián
make a boutique and well-crafted production of juicy Bonarda,
refreshing Criolla and now a white Criolla (Muscat). While Cara Sur
(southern face) makes reference to a tough climb that the Bugallo
brothers survived up a difficult mountain face, these wines are a
testimony to easy-drinking: fresh, vibrant and showing a whole new
face for Barreal's wine.

franciscobugallo@gmail.com
+54 9 264 464 8155
Pancho Bugallo

Bodega Miras

A well-established winemaker for Bodega Fin del Mundo, Marcelo

The vineyards at Ver Sacrum

Miras is by no means new on the circuit, but he is putting forward a fresh face with his son Pablo Miras in their family winery, Bodega Miras. Although a Mendoza native, Marcelo moved to Patagonia many years ago where his family grew up and he has become an expert in the Rio Negro region. Patagonia is a region that is well worth keeping your eye on for the future of Argentine winemaking, and Miras is a family winery which is already making fine exponents from the area that are long overdue some attention. Their growing collection includes an excellent Trousseau Nouveau (possibly the only one in Argentina), rich Semillon, attractive Chardonnay and herbal and fresh Cabernet Franc.

info@bodegamiras.com.ar

+54 299 581 7139
Marcelo or Pablo Miras
www.marcelomiras.com.ar

Finca Las Payas

A 'natural' winemaker in Argentina, Santiago Salgado moved out of the hustle and bustle of Buenos Aires to follow a countryside lifestyle in San Rafael where he has now been making wine since 2005, each year with increasing panache. Experimenting with less common varieties in Argentina like Nero D'Avola, Croatina, Crovina and Caladoc, and using minimal intervention techniques, his production is far from the ordinary in Argentina. There is a surprising line-up of different grape varieties, but the top wines to try are Ancelota from the Exotico range, Juanito Syrah and an orange wine made from Moscatel Rosado which comes with a rather captivating label.

autor@fincalaspayas.com.ar
+54 9 261 432 1942
Santiago Salgado
www.fincalaspayas.com.ar

Ver Sacrum

Although the winemakers are silent partners in the project, the wines speak for themselves. A brand new project experimenting with Mediterranean varieties in Mendoza, co-owner Eduardo Soler and his cronies are making Grenache, a GSM (Grenache-Syrah-Mourvedre) blend, and a Monstrell to date and in future vintages we'll undoubtedly see more. The potential of mediterranean varieties in is a hot topic in both Argentina and neighbouring Chile, but there are as of yet few producers to put their money where their mouth is, and Ver Sacrum is one of the first. With brand new vineyards in the Uco Valley and old vines in Maipu, San Juan and La Rioja, there is ample material to choose from. Word on the grapevine is that Roussane-Marsanne is next blend on their list to shake up the variety revolution currently happening in Argentina.

grenachista@gmail.com
+54 9 2616392757
Eduardo Soler

EAT AND SLEEP

The Mendoza province is Argentina's most prolific wine region, responsible for approximately two-thirds of the country's total wine production and famous for its Malbecs and bold reds. Considered the center of the winemaking industry in not just Argentina but all of Latin America, the area is also a top wine and food travel destination. Grape Collective highlights some of Mendoza's hotel and restaurant options.

HOTELS

Casa de Uco Vineyards & Wine Hotel
Ruta 94, km 14.5, 5500 Tunuyán, Mendoza, Argentina
+54 11 5245 5550
www.casadeuco.com

Intercontinental Mendoza
Pérez Cuesta, Mendoza, Argentina
+54 261 521-8800
www.ihg.com

Park Hyatt Mendoza
Chile 1124, Mendoza, Argentina, 5500
+54 261 441 1234
www.mendoza.park.hyatt.com

Alpasion Lodge
Ruta Provincial 94, Distrito los Chacayes, Tunuyán, 5500 Los Sauces, Argentina

104

+54 9 261 242-9689
www.alpasion.com

Cavas Wine Lodge
Costaflores s/n, Cobos, 5507 Luján de Cuyo, Mendoza, Argentina
+54 11 4312-8067
www.cavaswinelodge.com

Club Tapiz
Ruta 60 Km 2.5, Pedro Molina s/n, 5517 Russell, Maipú, Mendoza,
Argentina
+54 261 496-3433
www.tapiz.com

The Vines Resort & Spa
Ruta Provincial 94, km 11, 5565 Tunuyán, Mendoza, Argentina
+54 261 461-3900
www.vinesresortandspa.com

Posada Salentein
Ruta 89 s/n Finca La Pampa Los Arboles, 5560 Mendoza, Argentina
+54 2622 42 9000
www.bodegasalentein.com

RESTAURANTS

Siete Fuegos Asado
Ruta Provincial 94, km 11, Tunuyan, Uco Valley, Mendoza, Argentina
+54 261 461 3910
www.vinesresortandspa.com

Azafran
Av. Sarmiento 765, Mendoza, Argentina
+54 261 429-4200
www.azafranresto.com

Don Mario
25 de Mayo 1324, 5519 Mendoza, Argentina
+54 261 431-0810
www.donmario.com

Siete Cocinas
Av. Bartolomé Mitre 794, 5500 Mendoza, Argentina

+54 261 423-8823
www.sietecocinas.com

Ituzaingo Restó
1548 Ituzaingo St, Mendoza 5500, Argentina
+54 261 9 156665778
www.ituzaingoresto.com

Bistro M at Park Hyatt
Chile 1124, 5500 Mendoza, Argentina
+54 261 441-123
www.mendoza.park.hyatt.com

María Antonieta
Av. Belgrano 1069, 5500 Mendoza, Argentina
+54 261 420-4322
www.mariaantonietaresto.com

Finca Blousson
Ruta 94 km14 - Camino al Manzano Histórico, Tunuyán, Mendoza,
5560 Vista Flores, Mendoza, Argentina
+54 (261) 483-9250
www.fincablousson.com

Almacen de Uco
Ruta Provincial 89 s/n, Manzano Historico, Tunuyan, Mendoza,
Argentina
0262215679424
www.almacendeuco.com